Thinking Beyond the Content:
Critical Reading for Academic Success

Nolan J. Weil
Utah State University

Raymond Cepko
University of Tampa

Ann Arbor
University of Michigan Press

2011   2010   2009   2008   4   3   2   1

No part of this publication may be reproduced, stored in a retrieval system, or transmitted in any form or by any means, electronic, mechanical, or otherwise, without the written permission of the publisher.

ISBN-13: 978-0-472-08977-2

CONTENTS

ACKNOWLEDGMENTS

Grateful acknowledgment is given to the following authors, publishers, and individuals for permission to reprint previously published materials:

Bergin & Garvey for excerpts from *The Anthropology of Sport: An Introduction, Rev. Ed.,* by Kendall Blanchard, 1995.

Crown Publishers, Inc., for excerpts from "In a Time of Crisis" by Dave Foreman from *Confessions of an Eco-Warrior,* published by Harmony Books, 1991.

Doubleday & Company for excerpts from "Designing the Superman" by Isaac Asimov in *Science Past–Science Future,* 1975.

Foreign Affairs for excerpts from "The Human-Animal Link" by William B. Karesh and Robert A. Cook, Vol. 84, No. 4, July-August 2005.

Harcourt Brace Jovanovich for excerpts from "Form and Meaning in Natural Languages" by Noam Chomsky's *Language and Mind,* © 1972.

Jupiter Unlimited for photos.

Leisure Press for excerpts from "Sport: Work or Play?" by Allen L. Sack from *Studies in the Anthropology of Play: Papers in Memory of B. Allan Tindall,* edited by Phillip Stevens, Jr., 1977.

The New York Times Syndicate for "Approximating Life" by Clive Thompson, 7 July 2002.

Oryx Press for excerpts from "Information Overload" by Joan R. Callahan from *Oryx Frontiers of Science Series: Recent Advances and Issues in Environmental Science,* 2000.

Routledge for excerpts from "The Why of Sports" from *Making Sense of Sports, 2nd ed.,* by Ellis Cashmore, 2004.

Science for excerpts from "North Atlantic Right Whales in Crisis" by Scott D. Kraus et al. Vol. 309, July 22, 2005.

The World Bank for excerpts from *Curbing the Epidemic: Governments and the Economics of Tobacco Control,* 1999.

The World Health Organization for excerpts from *On Being an Adolescent in the 21st Century* by Paul F. A. Van Look, 2003.

Every effort has been made to contact the copyright holders for permission to reprint borrowed material. We regret any oversight that may have occurred and will rectify them in future printings of the book.

TO THE TEACHER

Thinking Beyond the Text: Critical Reading for Academic Success is aimed at advanced college or college-bound ESL readers, although developing readers at the college level whose native language is English could also profitably use it. It is a theme-based text with an academic focus designed not only to challenge its readers to read closely for understanding, but also to go beyond the literal content of a text and to engage in critical thinking and investigation. Our intention has been to produce a text that will serve as a suitable bridge between most of the ESL reading texts currently available and the texts used in the academic disciplines.

Deciding which themes and readings to include has required us to search, browse, and read extensively to identify compelling themes and associated readings that would balance a number of considerations. First, we have made an effort to select readings that we felt would be interesting and accessible to our readers while at the same time not minimizing challenge. Although we have included several articles from popular press sources, in general, we have strived to find readings more representative of academic media, while trying to avoid writing that we felt would be too technical or overly loaded with academic jargon.

We have also sought to include readings that are somewhat longer than those usually encountered in texts designed for ESL readers, although in some cases it has been necessary for us to abridge a reading when we felt its length was disproportionate to its companion articles. Of course, a number of selections are not self-contained articles at all but excerpts from book-length works. With these excerpts, it has been necessary to find convenient beginning and ending points without compromising the coherence of the excerpt; this was not always easy.

Finally, while not departing entirely from what have become traditional themes in anthologies intended for general education courses, we have nevertheless tried to give this book an original slant. For instance, Unit 2: Language and Being, straddles a number of disciplines, (i.e., artificial intelligence, linguistics, philosophy of mind) not often attempted in books such as this. Unit 4: Thinking About Sport avoids the usual celebrity approach in favor of an intellectually challenging journey into sport from an academic point of view.

We have successfully used many of the materials in this book with students enrolled in the English Language Institute at the University of South Florida and the Intensive English Language Institute at Utah State University. With few exceptions, the topics have generated enthusiasm, and students have found the readings and supporting exercises challenging and thought provoking.

Organization

Thinking Beyond the Text is organized into four thematic units consisting of three readings per unit.

- 1—Environmental Issues: a necessarily cursory glimpse of a broad field with global implications
- 2—Language and Being: an inquiry into the boundaries of language and human identity
- 3—Global Health Issues: an overview of some global challenges to public health
- 4—Thinking About Sport: critical reflections on the definition of sport and the excitement of competition

Features

Each unit consists of these components:

- **Overview.** Each unit opens with a brief overview of the general theme.
- **Readings.** The unit theme is developed through three related or topically linked readings.
- **Pre-Reading Questions.** Every reading is preceded by one or more pre-reading questions or activities designed to activate the reader's prior knowledge of the topic.
- **Vocabulary Glosses.** In an effort to reduce vocabulary-related barriers to fluent reading, glosses are provided for some lower-frequency vocabulary. Vocabulary for glossing was selected with the aid of the Web VP (VocabProfiler) at *www.lextutor.ca/vp/eng/*[1]. *Thinking Beyond the Text* is intended for the advanced ESL reader, and we assume readers will know the 2000 most frequently occurring English words as measured by a list such as the West List (West, 1953) as well as a high proportion of words in higher frequency bands. In using terms like higher and lower frequency, we do not mean to imply any scientifically rigorous threshold for defining frequency. Lower-frequency means only that glossed words are not among the 2000 most frequently occurring words, and based on our professional

---

[1] Web VP (maintained by Tom Cobb) code the vocabulary of a text as belonging to one of the following four categories: (1) the first 1,000 most frequent words on the General Service List (West, 1953), (2) the second 1,000 most frequent words, (3) the Academic Word List (AWL) composed of 570 word families found with high-frequency in academic texts (Coxhead, 2000), and (4) off-list words—meaning words that are neither among the 2,000 most frequent words nor among the 570 word families on the AWL. In *Thinking Beyond the Text*, all glossed vocabulary consists of off-list words.

To the Teacher

judgment a large percentage of student readers are not likely to be familiar with them.

- **Critical Focus.** Associated with most readings in the first three units is at least one academic reading/critical thinking strategy. Critical Focus boxes, explaining the strategy are usually positioned after the reading. Critical Focus advice is aimed at increasing a reader's ability to read and think critically about the content of a reading or follow up on it in some way. Unit 4 has only one new Critical Focus section, but several previously introduced skills are recycled.

- **Critical Focus Application.** Critical Focus boxes are followed by application tasks, which provide the reader an opportunity to use what has been presented within the context of the preceding reading selection.

- **Getting at the Matter.** Every reading has a section entitled Getting at the Matter, which consists of questions, tasks, or activities for enhancing comprehension of the main points of the reading.

- **Academic Vocabulary Focus.** Every reading is accompanied by a section that draws the reader's attention to a selection of vocabulary from Averil Coxhead's (2000) Academic Word List (AWL)[2]. Web VP was used to identify all academic vocabulary in each reading, and we have selected approximately 15 academic vocabulary items in each reading for special attention through a variety of exercises and activities. To select vocabulary items for each unit, we first developed a database of all academic words in each reading. We then used the database to identify overlap in the occurrence of particular items across readings (ignoring the possibility that the same word could be used in different senses) and tried to select items in such a way as to give the widest coverage without exceeding 15 words per reading. We have limited the selection to 15 because in our experience, students tend to feel overwhelmed when confronted with vocabulary lists that are much longer.

- **For Discussion.** Suggestions for discussion, many of which can be carried out either through writing or conversation, accompany each reading. Discussion allows readers to elaborate on content, extend the themes through reflection on personal associations, or work on developing written and oral fluency through response to the readings.

- **For Further Investigation.** Each unit ends with this section; here readers will find suggestions for follow-up tasks and research projects through which they can explore connections between readings or learn more about writers, sources, organizations, or aspects of a topic mentioned in the readings.

---

[2] Coxhead's AWL can be accessed at *http://language.massey.ac.nz/staff/awl/index.shtml.*

In general, the components are ordered in the same way throughout the book; however, the placement of the **Critical Focus** section may differ from one reading to another because we have placed it where we feel it best complements the other components of a reading. For instance, in Unit 3, it makes more sense to position **Previewing a Text** before rather than after the reading. In Unit 2, we have placed the **Critical Focus: Comparing Points of View** after rather before the **Getting at the Matter** discussion, a reversal of our usual practice, because it makes sense to discuss singly all points of view that will be involved in a comparison before moving on to compare various points of view. However, in many cases there is no reason why you could not reverse the order of these sections.

The placement of **Academic Vocabulary Focus** is also somewhat arbitrary. Although we have positioned it after **Getting at the Matter** and before **For Discussion,** there is no reason why it could not immediately follow the reading. We invite students and instructors to decide when the right time is to focus on the selected **Academic Vocabulary Focus** section.

REFERENCES

Coxhead, A. (2000). A new academic word list. *TESOL Quarterly, 34*(2), 213–238.

West, M. (1953). *A general service list of English words.* London: Longman, Green & Company.

TO THE STUDENT

Thinking Beyond the Text: Critical Reading for Academic Success was designed to help you move beyond literal understanding of a text and to encourage you to exercise higher-order thinking of the sort that is increasingly valued in post-secondary academic settings. The book has four units, each with a different theme explored from different points of view through three readings. We have chosen readings we feel will be academically challenging for more advanced learners of English and yet still accessible. You will probably need to read each selection more than one time to fully comprehend the content. However, you should be aware that this is a common practice for many native speakers when they encounter readings that contain new information or information that is more complex than they are used to.

Academic reading is not a passive activity. To be a good academic reader, you must read actively, critically, and deeply. This book is designed to teach you some techniques for doing that. Throughout your reading, you will want to highlight important information and make marginal notes because, unlike reading for pleasure, reading for academic purposes requires you to remember important information for later use. You will also want to write any questions that the reading might provoke in preparation for doing further research on the subject. You can either highlight and make marginal notes on your first reading or on subsequent readings as you begin to understand the text more clearly. Either way, you will want to practice these strategies with the readings in this book so they come naturally when you are in the university or college classroom.

Each reading begins with a **Pre-Reading** activity to start you thinking about the topic or topics that you will encounter. If you are in a class with other students, your teacher may ask you to work together with a small group of classmates on some of the activities. At other times, you may be asked to work on your own. You might be be asked to share your ideas with the rest of the class or engage in some form of group discussion. Thinking about and discussing the topic with others activates any background knowledge you may have about the topic, and this will help you be better prepared to process any new information and vocabulary that may be contained in the reading.

After each reading, you will encounter several post-reading activities. First, you will generally be presented with a **Critical Focus** that will help you understand some important elements to look for in academic texts. This advice is then followed by a **Critical Focus Application** to give you an opportunity to use what you are learning. At times you will be challenged to apply a previously learned strategy in a more complex manner as you progress through the book.

The **Getting at the Matter** section is designed to check your comprehension of key ideas and important details in each reading. Sometimes these questions will require you to include information you gathered in the strategy section that preceded it; however, you will usually be asked to present the information in complete sentences and in your own words. The **Academic Vocabulary Focus** will help you increase your academic vocabulary by focusing on 176 words from the 570 word families that are commonly found within academic writing across the various disciplines. A variety of activities will help you with recognition of this vocabulary and reinforce your ability to recognize or use it in context.

An important aspect of American higher education is the application and extension of knowledge as well as the questioning of it. **For Discussion** sections will help you move beyond the information gathered from the text by having you explore your personal responses to what you have read, to think of further applications and implications of ideas from the readings, or to think of objections and criticisms of those ideas. In addition, at the end of each unit is a **For Further Investigation** section. Here, you will be invited to do further research and present the information that you find either in oral or written form. This is important because doing research and synthesizing information from various sources is an important aspect of a college student's academic life. This is your opportunity to begin practicing advanced scholarship and to contribute new insights related to the material in this book—to go beyond the text.

1: Environmental Issues

Ever since human beings first appeared on Earth, they have altered the natural environment, sometimes depleting the resources they depend on for survival. However, during the 20th century, the influence of humans on the environment was unprecedented in its global reach by comparison with previous centuries. Now in these early years of the 21st century, the industrialized societies of the world are already on the way to making the 20th century look like an age of moderation.

This unit's first reading, "In Time of Crisis," is an excerpt from a book by Dave Foreman, an environmental activist and writer committed to wildlife conservation. Foreman argues that Earth is headed for an ecological disaster. He warns that to avoid self-destruction, humanity must adopt an environmental ethic based on a deep recognition that all life is interconnected.

In the second reading, "Information Overload," zoologist and environmental science writer Joan R. Callahan blames the media for exaggerating claims of impending doom, and she suggests that many environmental concerns may be greatly exaggerated.

In the third reading, "North Atlantic Right Whales in Crisis," a team of 16 researchers, including marine biologists, ecologists, and oceanographers, presents evidence of the decline of North Atlantic right whales as a result of human activities and proposes measures for preventing the further decline of the right whale population.

Reading 1

Pre-Reading

Write one paragraph in response to each question. Then share what you have written with a partner.

1. The title of Reading 1 is "In Time of Crisis." What is a **crisis**? Give an example of a crisis and describe how you would respond to that crisis.

2. Are there environmental issues you think are serious enough to be called crises? Explain.

3. Notice that the article you are about to read was first published in 1991 but reprinted in an environmental studies book in 2000. Why might that be? What might it say about the content of the reading?

Dave Foreman

This article originally appeared in Confessions of an eco-warrior. *(1991). New York: Harmony Books. Reprinted in Goldfarb, T. D. (Ed.), (2000).* Notable selections in environmental studies (2nd ed.), *pp. 361-362. Guilford, CT: Dushkin/McGraw Hill.*

Dave Foreman is an environmental writer and strong advocate of wildlife conservation. He was one of the founders of Earth First, a controversial environmental group that emerged in the 1980s and published a journal by the same name. When the original Earth First split apart in 1990, Foreman went on to co-found the Wildlands Project and launch the journal *Wild Earth*. While Earth First emphasized direct personal action in defense of the environment, the Wildlands Project is more committed to a strategy of shaping environmental policy through principles of conservation biology.

Although originally published in 1991, Foreman's essay, *In Time of Crisis,* remains as relevant today as it was when first published. If anything, the main problem that Foreman addresses, the loss of species, has become even more serious today than it was in 1991. In 2004, Foreman published a book entitled *Rewilding North America: A Vision for Conservation in the 21st Century* in which he addresses the issue of species loss and provides more detailed evidence for the claims he made in his 1991 book.

It is important when reading an older article, such as *In Time of Crisis,* to keep the publication date in mind. As you read, notice the use of time-reference words such as *now, today* and *recently*. Don't forget that these words do not literally refer to *now, today,* and *recently* when you are reading the article many years after its original publication. Much of the reading assigned to students in college and university classes will be as up to date as possible, but older readings are sometimes assigned to put an idea or issue in historical context. As a critical reader, you will want to think about the ways in which such articles are or are not of continuing relevance.

1   We are living now in the most critical moment in the three-and-a-half-billion-year history of life on Earth. For this unimaginably long time, life has been developing, expanding, blossoming, and diversifying, filling every available niche[1] with different manifestations[2] of itself, intertwined in complex, globe-girdling[3] relationships. But today this diversity of perhaps 30 million species faces radical and unprecedented change. Never before—not even during the mass extinctions of the dinosaurs at the end of the Cretaceous era, 65 million years ago—has there been such a high rate of extinction as we are now witnessing, such a drastic reduction in the planet's biological diversity.

2   Over the last three or four hundred years, human civilization has declared war on large mammals, leading some respected ecologists to assert that the only large mammals living twenty years from now will be those we humans choose to allow to live. Other prominent biologists, looking aghast[4] on the wholesale devastation of tropical rain forests and temperate-zone old-growth forests, rapidly accelerating desertification, rapacious[5] commercial fishing, and wasting of high-profile large mammals like whales, elephants, and tigers ("charismatic megafauna") owing to habitat destruction and poaching, say Earth could lose one-quarter to one-third of all species within forty years.

3   Not only is this blitzkrieg against the natural world destroying ecosystems and their associated species, but our activities are now beginning to have fundamental, systematic effects upon the entire life-support apparatus[6] of the planet: upsetting the world's climate; poisoning the oceans; destroying the atmospheric ozone layer that protects us from excessive ultraviolet radiation; changing the CO_2 ratio in the atmosphere and causing the "greenhouse effect"; and spreading acid rain, radioactive fallout[7], pesticides, and industrial contamination throughout the biosphere. Indeed, Professor Michael Soule, founder of the Society for Conservation Biology, recently warned that vertebrate evolution may be at an end due to the activities of industrial humans.

4   Clearly, in such a time of crisis, the conservation battle is not one of merely protecting outdoor recreation opportunities, or a matter of aesthetics[8], or "wise management and use" of natural resources. It is a battle for life itself, for the continued flow of evolution. We—this generation of humans—are at our most important juncture since we came out of the trees six million years ago. It is our decision, ours today, whether Earth continues

---

[1] niche: an area or space where something fits
[2] manifestations: appearances, signs
[3] globe-girdling: encircling the earth
[4] aghast: shocked
[5] rapacious: greedy
[6] life-support apparatus: the biological processes that support life on Earth
[7] radioactive fallout: poisonous and usually deadly dust that is created when a nuclear bomb explodes
[8] aesthetics: pleasing appearance or beauty

to be a marvelously living, diverse oasis in the blackness of space, or whether the "charismatic megafauna" of the future will consist of Norway Rats and cockroaches.

5   How have we arrived at this state, at this threshold of biotic terror? Is it because we have forgotten our "place in nature," as the Native American activist Russell Means says?

6   If there is one thing upon which the nation states of the world today can agree, one thing at which the United States and the Soviet Union, Israel and Iran, South Africa and Angola, Britain and Argentina, China and India, Japan and Malaysia nod in unison, it is that human beings are the measure of all value. As Gifford Pinchot, founder of the United States Forest Service, said, there are only two things on Earth: human beings and natural resources. Humanism is the philosophy that runs the business engines of the modern world.

7   The picture that most humans have of the natural world is that of a smorgasbord table, continually replenished by a magic kitchen hidden somewhere in the background. While most people perceive that there are gross and immoral inequities[9] in the sizes of the plates handed out and in the number of times some are allowed to belly up to the bar, few of us question whether the items arrayed are there for their sole use, nor do they imagine that the table will ever become empty.

8   There is another way to think about man's relationship to the natural world, an insight pioneered by the nineteenth-century conservationist and mountaineer John Muir and later by the science of ecology. This is the idea that all things are connected, interrelated, that human beings are merely one of the millions of species that have been shaped by the process of evolution for three and a half billion years. According to this view, all living beings have the same right to be here. This is how I see the world.

9   With that understanding, we can answer the question, "Why wilderness?"

10   Is it because wilderness makes pretty picture postcards? Because it protects watersheds for downstream use by agriculture, industry, and homes? Because it's a good place to clean the cobwebs out of our heads after a long week in the auto factory or over the video display terminal? Because it preserves resource-extraction opportunities for the future generations of humans? Because some unknown plant living in the wilds may hold a cure for cancer?

11   No—the answer is, because wilderness is. Because it is the real world, the flow of life, the process of evolution, the repository of that three and a half billion years of shared travel.

12   A Grizzly Bear snuffling[10] along Pelican Creek in Yellowstone National Park with her two cubs has just as much right to life as any human has, and is far more important ecologically. All things have intrinsic value[11], inherent worth. Their value is not determined

---

[9] inequities: unfair or unequal situations

[10] snuffling: sniffing or rapidly breathing air in and out of the nose to aid in smelling something

[11] intrinsic value: having worth in itself and not because of its usefulness

Thinking Beyond the Content

by what they will ring up on the cash register of the gross national product, or by whether or not they are *good*. They are good because they exist.

13   Even more important than the individual wild creature is the wild community—the wilderness, the stream of life unimpeded[12] by human manipulation.

14   We, as human beings, as members of industrial civilization, have no divine mandate[13] to pave, conquer, control, develop, or use every square inch of this planet. As Edward Abbey, author of *Desert Solitaire* and *The Monkey Wrench Gang*, said, we have a right to be here, yes, but not everywhere, all at once.

15   The preservation of wilderness is not simply a question of balancing competing special-interest groups, arriving at a proper mix of uses on our public lands, and resolving conflicts between different outdoor recreation preferences. It is an ethical and moral matter. A religious mandate. Human beings have stepped beyond the bounds; we are destroying the very process of life.

16   The forest ranger and wilderness proponent Aldo Leopold perhaps stated this ethic best: *A thing is right when it tends to preserve the integrity, stability, and beauty of the biotic community. It is wrong when it tends otherwise.*

---

[12] unimpeded: free
[13] divine mandate: official command or order from God

Critical Focus: Identifying the Tone of a Text

Tone refers to those qualities in a piece of writing that show the writer's feeling about the subject. Academic communities generally value texts that are objective and balanced. They also tend to expect arguments to be based on reason rather than strong emotion. Being sensitive to the tone of a text not only helps a reader better understand the writer's attitude toward the subject, it can also help the critical reader evaluate the writer's argument as we will soon show.

In speech, tone may be easy to recognize because the listener can pay attention to the way that the speaker says something as well as the words the speaker uses. For example, the speaker's tone of voice may reveal whether a speaker feels cheerful or disappointed, excited or bored, angry or amused. But identifying the tone of a text is harder. To determine the tone of a piece of writing, a reader must rely entirely on language.

A number of elements in the writer's language can contribute to tone, including: the length and structure of sentences, the use of vivid imagery, and the kinds of details the writer uses. But the writer's choice of words is probably the single most important element of tone. Sometimes the writer's choice of words suggests some positive or negative associations beyond the literal meaning of the words. When a writer uses language that seems designed to produce strong emotional reactions in the reader, the critical reader should probably question the writer's objectivity.

Here is an example from Paragraph 2 of *In Time of Crisis:*
> Over the last three or four hundred years, human civilization has **declared war** on large mammals. . . .

Here is the same passage rewritten by one of the authors of this book.
> Over the last three or four hundred years, human activity **has lead to a troubling decline in many species** of large mammals. . . .

How is the tone of the second passage different from that of the original passage? What word choices contribute to the difference?

For one thing, the use of the phrase *has declared war on* is quite negative, **accusing** humans of purposely trying to destroy all the large mammals as if they were dangerous enemies. If we wish to describe the tone of the original passage, we might say it has an **accusatory** tone.

On the other hand, the second passage is much more moderate and cautious in tone. The phrase *human activity has lead to a troubling decline* expresses the idea that large mammals are decreasing in number. The phrase *many species* suggests that the statement is true of some—although perhaps not all—large mammals. Furthermore, the second passage admits that human beings are responsible for the decline, but it does not imply that they have done it on purpose. The use of the word *troubling* still suggests that the writer thinks this is a problem that should be of concern to humans. So it does not hide the writer's opinion, but it does so in a way that is **more balanced** and **more objective.** If we were to describe the tone, we might say it expresses **concern.**

To summarize, tone is a clue that can help the critical reader determine the writer's attitude toward the subject. A tone that is overly emotional might lead the reader to question a writer's objectivity, cautioning the reader to be extra careful about accepting the writer's conclusions.

Let's conclude by reviewing two strategies a critical reader can use to become more aware of a writer's tone. They are the strategies we have used to analyze the two passages from the preceding example:

1. Ask yourself what feeling the writer seems to be conveying (either throughout the whole text or in shorter passages). Try to find an adjective that describes that feeling. For help with this, see the list of useful adjectives that can be used to describe the tone of a text.

2. Try to look for words and phrases that seem to suggest associations that go beyond the literal meanings of the words.

Some Useful Adjectives for Describing the Tone of a Text

Here is a brief list of words to help you begin developing a vocabulary to describe tone. You will want to look up words that you are not familiar with in a dictionary and add new words to the list as you learn more.

abstract	accusatory	angry	alarmed
bitter	boring	calm	cheerful
cold	compassionate	concerned	confident
contemptuous	critical	cynical	distressed
dramatic	factual	formal	humorous
impartial	impassioned	indifferent	indignant
inflammatory	informal	ironic	mocking
objective	pretentious	proud	restrained
sarcastic	sentimental	skeptical	subjective
surprised	sympathetic	upset	urgent

Critical Focus: Application

With a partner, discuss these questions related to the tone of Reading 1.

1. How would you describe the writer's tone in Paragraph 1? Which words help you determine this? What adjective from the list in the Critical Focus box on page 9 would you use to describe the tone of this paragraph?

2. What does the word *blitzkrieg* mean in Paragraph 3? What do you think is implied by the use of this word? What adjective would you use to describe the tone of this paragraph?

3. What adjective would you use to describe the tone of Paragraph 7? What words help you to determine the tone? Identify and discuss language that seems designed to present the reader with a mental picture.

4. What does the phrase *divine mandate* in Paragraph 14 mean? What do you think is implied by the use of this phrase? What adjective would you use to describe the tone of this paragraph?

5. How would you describe the overall tone of this article? Use one or more of the adjectives from the table of useful adjectives on page 9.

Getting at the Matter

Answer the questions in writing. Then discuss your responses with one or more partners.

1. In Reading 1, the writer claims that we are living in a time of crisis. What does he mean? Explain the main ideas of the reading in your own words.

2. What evidence does the writer offer to support the claim that we are living in a time of crisis? If necessary, reread the article and note the details he uses to support his claim.

3. The writer also puts forward an environmental ethic based on his view of man's relationship to the natural world. (An *ethic* is a theory of "right and wrong.") What is the writer's view of the human being's place in the natural world? Explain in your own words the ethical principle behind the writer's position.

4. The writer clearly values wilderness. According to the author, what is wilderness? How would you define it?

5. The writer mentions a number of possible reasons why wilderness should be protected, but he finds only one legitimate reason. What reasons does he reject, and what reason does he support?

Thinking Beyond the Content

Academic Vocabulary Focus

Using a dictionary and a word map (a visually interesting way of representing new vocabulary) can be useful vocabulary learning strategies for some students. **Dictionaries** provide more than definitions. They also indicate the part of speech of a word, the pronunciation, examples of how a word is used, synonyms and/or antonyms for the word, and a short list of other forms of the word. Online dictionaries like Merriam-Webster also allow you to hear the word pronounced.

For example, if you look up the word *critical* in the Merriam-Webster Online Dictionary *(www.m-w.com),* you will see this information:

Main Entry: **crit·i·cal** 🔊

Pronunciation: 'kri-ti-kəl

Function: *adjective*

1a: of, relating to, or being a turning point or specially important juncture <a *critical* phase>: as (1) : relating to or being the stage of a disease at which an abrupt change for better or worse may be expected; *also* : being or relating to an illness or condition involving danger of death <*critical* care> <a patient listed in *critical* condition> (2) : relating to or being a state in which or a measurement or point at which some quality, property, or phenomenon suffers a definite change <*critical* temperature> **b:** CRUCIAL, DECISIVE <a *critical* test> **c:** INDISPENSABLE, VITAL <a *critical* waterfowl habitat> <a component *critical* to the operation of a machine> **d:** being in or approaching a state of crisis <a *critical* shortage> <a *critical* situation>

- **crit·i·cal·i·ty** 🔊/'kri-tə-'ka-lə-tē/ *noun*
- **crit·i·cal·ly** 🔊/'kri-ti-k(ə-)lē/ *adverb*
- **crit·i·cal·ness** 🔊/-kəl-nəs/ *noun*

A **word map** is a way of visualizing the various important features of a word. Visual learners might find this to be an effective way to record, study, and learn new vocabulary. Word maps can be drawn by hand on paper or index cards or created on a computer screen using drawing tools. A sample format for a word map follows.

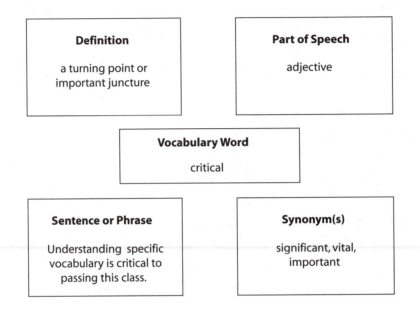

Thinking Beyond the Content

In the chart that follows are 15 words from the Academic Word List (AWL) that appear in the reading "In Time of Crisis."

1. Scan the reading for the words, and write the number of the paragraph where the word *first* appears.

diversity (Par.)	ethical (Par.)	extraction (Par. 10)	inherent (Par.)	integrity (Par.)
insight (Par.)	intrinsic (Par.)	manipulation (Par.)	perceive (Par.)	philosophy (Par.)
ratio (Par.)	register (Par.)	sole (Par.)	terminal (Par.)	unprecedented (Par.)

2. Next, look up each word in a dictionary. Be careful because several of the words have more than one meaning; you may need to double-check how the word is used in the reading to get the correct definition. Use the meaning that matches how the word is used in the reading.

3. Create word maps for at least six of the vocabulary items. If you find word mapping useful, you may wish to do it routinely as a word study strategy.

For Discussion

Discuss these questions with a partner or small group.

1. The writer focuses exclusively on the negative impact that humans have had on the environment. Are there any ways in which human activity positively has affected the environment? On balance, do you think the environmental effect of human activity is positive or negative?

2. In Paragraph 2, the writer refers to *charismatic megafauna* such as whales, elephants, and tigers. Wildlife conservationists often find it easy to mobilize public sentiment for these endangered *megafauna*. It might be much more difficult to arouse public sympathy for a creature such as an insect or a worm. Do you believe that some species are more important to protect than others? Or do you feel that even the smallest and most insignificant species is worth saving? Explain your opinion.

3. Describe the environmental ethic (i.e., the set of principles of right and wrong in relation to human interaction with nature) that you think people should live by.

Reading 2

Pre-Reading

Respond to the questions; then discuss your responses with one or more classmates.

1. What do you think of when you hear or read the term *toxic chemicals*? Can you name any toxic chemicals? Which of these statements comes closest to expressing your belief about toxic chemicals in the environment?

    ____ a. They are a significant threat to my health.

    ____ b. I am not exposed to toxic chemicals, so they are not a significant threat to my health.

    ____ c. I do not know if toxic chemicals are a threat to my health.

2. What is *biotechnology*? Can you give any examples of current applications of biotechnology? Which of these statements comes closest to expressing your belief about biotechnology?

    ____ a. It is a significant threat to my health.

    ____ b. I am not exposed to biotechnology, so it is not a significant threat to my health.

    ____ c. I do not know if biotechnology is a threat to my health.

Joan R. Callahan

From Callahan, J. R. (2000). Recent advances and issues in environmental science. *Phoenix, AZ: The Oryx Press, 179–184.*

As this textbook goes to press, we are barely into the 21st century. *Information Overload,* an excerpt from a book published in 2000, provides a good overview of how the environmental landscape appeared to science writer Joan Callahan as the world entered the 21st century. Callahan highlights the role of news media in keeping the public informed of environmental developments. In particular, she emphasizes the confusion and uncertainty that the ordinary citizen may feel when confronted with contradictory claims coming from government agencies, business organizations, environmental groups, and private citizens.

The particular environmental issues that receive the most intense news coverage sometimes change over the course of several years. Some issues come to the forefront, and others fade into the background only to return to center stage at a later time. The concerns that Callahan discussed in 2000 have not gone away, and they are unlikely to go away any time soon although the major newsmakers may change.

As you read *Information Overload,* think about what issues are currently receiving the most attention in the media. How are the current issues similar to the issues Callahan discusses, and how are they different? Notice also the difference in the tone of this reading in contrast to *In Time of Crisis.* Try to apply the strategies you learned for analyzing the tone of a text to this reading. What adjective(s) would you use to characterize Callahan's tone? Do any of her word choices seem to suggest associations that go beyond the literal meanings of the words?

1   The twentieth century's "information explosion" is a major social issue, and much of its shrapnel[14] is environmentally related. A century ago, the main topics of polite conversation at social gatherings were the weather and everyone's health. These topics have persisted[15], but with a new spin: disaster.

2   Today's environmental health and meteorological[16] news is largely negative and never-ending. Even office workers who rarely venture[17] outdoors have these issues piped directly to their living rooms or work stations, courtesy of the news media: deformed frogs in the local reservoir, unexplained outbreaks of some ghastly[18] disease, forests destroyed by an invading beetle, fish so full of mercury they could serve as thermometers, radon[19] seeping invisibly into our basements. Sooner or later, for many people, this constant barrage of doom[20] becomes intolerable.

3   As discussed earlier in this book, recent survey results indicate that people in the United States have begun to lose confidence in the goals of environmental protection, or at least in the government's ability to achieve those goals. Some observers believe that these attitudes stem from sheer[21] information overload. So many problems are competing for our attention that, like Scarlett[22], we would prefer to think about them tomorrow. The resulting fear, denial, and apathy may hamper[23] effective environmental planning, thus compounding the original problems.

Note: In Paragraph 3, Callahan is referring to her book, *Recent Advance and Issues in Environmental Science* from which the excerpt, *Information Overload*, was taken. Remember, too, that time words like *recent* are a reference to when the article was first written, not to when you are reading it.

Fear of Environmental Toxins

4   The environment is filled with hazardous chemicals, of both natural and artificial origin, and we hear about these dangers constantly. The existence of a hazard, however, does not necessarily imply a risk. It becomes a risk only if people are exposed to it in a way that can cause harm. People express their anxieties about these hazards in various ways, often in the guise[24] of humor. In the United States, at least, public confidence in the government's ability to deal with these issues appears to be at an all-time low.

5   In the mid-1980s, the town of Fallbrook, California, was in an uproar over certain chemicals allegedly[25] stored at a nearby U.S. Naval Weapons Station. Some of the residents claimed that the Navy was concealing thousands of leaking drums of nerve agents.

---

[14] shrapnel: fragments or small pieces from an explosive
[15] persisted: continued
[16] meteorological: having to do with the study of the earth's atmosphere and weather patterns
[17] venture: make a dangerous trip
[18] ghastly: very unpleasant or terrible
[19] radon: a type of radioactive chemical element
[20] barrage of doom: repeated messages of death and destruction
[21] sheer: complete
[22] Scarlett: a reference to Scarlett O'Hara, a character from the movie "Gone with the Wind"
[23] hamper: interfere with
[24] guise: something that conceals or hides
[25] allegedly: claimed but not proven

Thinking Beyond the Content

It seemed that every miscarriage[26], skin rash, or stomachache was blamed on the mysterious chemicals. In fact, the source of the rumors was a field containing 35,000 aging canisters of napalm–not nerve agent, but gasoline combined with benzene and polystyrene[27]. This material is flammable, and carelessly stored napalm has been known to catch fire in hot weather, but it is not particularly dangerous otherwise. Benzene, a carcinogen[28], is also present at lower levels in ordinary gasoline. Between 1979 and 1999, the Navy hired at least four contractors to dispose[29] of the napalm, but in each case, something went wrong. No matter where the Navy proposed to send the material for processing, the community objected. Finally, in 1999, disposal appeared to be in progress. The point is that no government conspiracy was involved. Federal contracting is a slow, inefficient process, and the risk was never that great anyway. At latest word, no one has produced evidence of an excess of cancers or any other disease in the Fallbrook area.

6   But why should people believe such explanations? No one really knows the effects of long-term exposure to certain environmental toxins at low levels; less than 5 percent of graduating medical students in the United States have had any environmental training. Even the effects of highly publicized toxic chemicals remain controversial after years of study. For example, scientists have long regarded PCBs as among the most hazardous environmental pollutants. Government agencies and businesses have spent millions of dollars cleaning up river and ocean sediments[30] contaminated with PCBs[31]. Then, in 1999, General Electric surprised us all with the results of a study of 7,000 people who worked with PCBs from 1946 to 1977. Although many of the subjects had high levels of PCBs in their blood, the death rates from cancer and other diseases were no higher than the general population. In 1977, a study of 25,000 persons had shown the opposite: those who developed lymphoma[32] had elevated levels of PCBs.

7   Many governments and industries have endangered people's lives at one time or another by underestimating risks. Chernobyl, Three Mile Island, Love Canal, Minimata Bay, Bikini Atoll–these are examples from history. More recently, the U.S. National Institute of Environmental Health and Sciences has acknowledged that many people who live near contaminated Department of Energy sites suffer from unexplained illnesses. In Canada, residents in Sydney, Nova Scotia, have asked why the death rate in their community is so high. Many blame Sydney Tar Ponds, a local toxic

---

[26] miscarriage: the premature death and discharge from the body of a human fetus
[27] polystyrene: a type of synthetic material
[28] carcinogen: a cancer-causing substance
[29] dispose: to get rid of
[30] sediments: material that settles at the bottom of a liquid when it is left standing
[31] PCBs: polychlorinated byphenyls; toxic chemicals that may accumulate in animal tissues
[32] lymphoma: a type of cancer

waste site, for the unusually high incidences[33] of cancer and other diseases, but clear evidence is lacking.

8   In a scenario similar to Fallbrook, a U.S. company (Thiokol Propulsion) recently helped Russian companies dispose of 30,000 tons of ballistic missile[34] fuel that was leaking from its storage containers near two towns. The health effects of this exposure are unknown. And, in Somerset, England, a farmer's environmental health claims were finally vindicated[35] after 10 years of conflict. The British Ministry of Agriculture had ignored the farmer's statements that overuse of an organophosphate pesticide had caused Britain's epidemic of mad cow disease (bovine spongiform encephalopathy, or BSE). The government had even prosecuted him for refusing to use the pesticide on his own cattle. The farmer claimed to be the target of death threats and arson[36], and was generally dismissed as a crank[37]. Then, in 1998, laboratory studies showed that the pesticide in question could, in fact, have made cattle highly susceptible to BSE. Some scientists now believe that BSE has always been present in cattle at a very low level.

9   "Reverse denial" also happens, and it does not inspire public confidence either. In 1998, health officials in Sydney, Australia, found what they believed to be extremely high levels of cryptosporidium (a waterborne parasite) in the city's water supply, and ordered all residents to boil their drinking water. Although not everyone complied, no one became ill. Some scientists later told the press that the organisms in the water were harmless algae, not cryptosporidium.

Fear of Biotechnology

10   Ben and Jerry's ice cream is delicious, but a generation ago, even a biochemist would have scratched her head at the statement on the carton:

> We oppose recombinant bovine growth hormone. The family farmers who supply our milk and cream pledge not to treat their cows with rBGH. The FDA has said no significant difference has been shown and no test can now distinguish between milk from RBGH treated and untreated cows. Not all of the suppliers of our other ingredients can promise that the milk they use comes from untreated cows.

11   The fact that Ben and Jerry's has gone to the trouble of printing all this information on its containers proves that consumers are interested. At present, the United States is the only developed nation in the world that allows dairy farmers to use rBGH. There is

---

[33] incidences: occurrences
[34] ballistic missile: a rocket that can be fired at an enemy
[35] vindicated: shown to be correct
[36] arson: the burning of a building or property for criminal reasons
[37] crank: a person with unusual ideas or opinions

no clear evidence that this practice is harmful, but people want reassurance. Both the "organic" food industry and its customer base have come a long way since the 1960s when health food dealers got away with outrageous claims. Today's consumers are better informed and demand accuracy.

12   The widespread interest in this subject was further demonstrated in 1998, when the U.S. Department of Agriculture (USDA) published its proposed standards for "organic" foods and requested public comment. The USDA promptly received nearly 30,000 letters, the most it had ever received as the result of such a notice. Many of the letters focused on three issues: food grown in sewage sludge[38], food treated with radiation, and biochemical foods. The USDA decided to exclude all three from the "organic" category, but postponed its final rule and asked for even more public feedback on three more points: animal confinement, animal medications, and certification procedures.

13   Despite this heightened consumer awareness, or perhaps because of it, biotechnology has come under fire. A generation ago, many people raised similar objections to irradiated[39] food and fluoridated drinking water. Today, the issue is genetically modified food. People have accepted bioengineered drugs such as insulin for years, but even that idea was not popular at first. In 1981, an Arizona minister gave an impassioned sermon on the future of biotechnology, starting with the words: "If those scientists get their way, some day you'll have a tree growing out of your head." More recently, British scientist Derek Burks said in an interview: "Genetic modification is becoming a sort of lightening rod for a whole series of late 20th century concerns." (1)

14   Both pro-environmental and anti-environmental groups have expressed doubts about biotechnology, although for different reasons. Even developing nations, whose people are hungry, have not entirely embraced the idea. Some of the most frequent concerns are as follows:

- rBGH (bovine growth hormone or bovine somatotropin) is a genetically engineered drug that makes dairy cows give more milk. When the U.S. Food and Drug Administration approved rBGH in 1993, it may have disregarded certain potential health risks. Although there is no clear evidence that milk produced in this manner is harmful, the U.S. Department of Health and Human Services is investigating the matter.
- Some crop plants that have been genetically modified to resist herbicides[40] might outcross with their wild relatives, producing hybrid weeds that would be nearly impossible to kill. Danish researchers have achieved this outcome experimentally

(1) Quoted in Reaney, P. (1998, September 10). Genetically altered plants safe, say UK Scientists. Reuters News Service.

---

[38] sludge: a muddy deposit of human waste
[39] irradiated: treated with radiation
[40] herbicides: poisons used to kill unwanted plants

using herbicide-resistant canola; scientists at the University of Chicago have warned that corn can outcross with a common weed called timothy grass.

- Edible crop plants that have been modified to produce their own built-in pesticides do not sound appetizing to many. Although many consumers are already eating such products without knowing it, this issue requires clarification.

- Individuals, consumer groups, and entire nations have questioned the need for genetically altered crops. In 1998, representatives from 24 African states told the UN Food and Agriculture Organization (FAO) that biotechnology is not the answer to world hunger. As they pointed out, there is already enough food in the world; poor people simply can't afford to buy it.

- Some crops, such as a new strain[41] of corn, have been genetically modified to resist antibiotics. Consumers have reasonably asked if eating this corn might interfere with the action of the antibiotics in the body.

- Consumers worry about possible allergic reactions to unexpected substances in foods. For example, one strain of soybean has an added gene from the Brazil nut. Many people are allergic to Brazil nuts, and eating those soybeans might make a person seriously ill.

- Finally, there is evidence that some genetically engineered plants may be harmful to animals. A controversial 1999 study showed that monarch butterfly caterpillars grew poorly after eating leaves dusted with pollen from transgenic corn.

15 Aside from these biologically based concerns, many people voiced ethical objections to the whole idea of genetic modification of living organisms, particularly animals. For example, several organizations are developing transgenic[42] fish with enhanced growth rates, disease resistance, or cold tolerance. Of this plan, activist Patricia Dines wrote: "We kill the existing fish with pollution, then want to replace them with corporate products, feeling we can engineer better than God. Is there value to preserving wild fish instead?" (2) 2 Others have protested current research on new contraceptive[43] techniques that would involve the actual genetic modification of human sperm and egg cells. Although the world needs safer, more convenient birth control methods, many mainstream scientists and physicians, as well as environmental activists, have asked if this is really the way to go.

16 These and similar objections are hard to ignore, and the biotechnology industry must find answers. In some cases, however, opponents have made outlandish[44]

---

(2) Sustainable Agriculture Network SANet e-mail list (1997, June 1).

---

[41] strain: a variety of an organism

[42] transgenic: plant or animal with some genes from a different species

[43] contraceptive: something used to prevent pregnancy

[44] outlandish: peculiar, strange

Thinking Beyond the Content

claims. Britain's Prince Charles has accused biotechnology firms of "playing God," when in reality they are just trying to profit from their research investment, and possibly making some mistakes along the way. Groups such as Greenpeace[45] regularly invade experimental fields, uproot some crop they find objectionable, and dump it with grand flourish on the doorstep of a corporation or embassy. (Ironically, this tactic has recently forced the British government to reconsider its policy of publishing the locations of genetic crop trials, thus replacing an atmosphere of openness with one of secrecy.) Greenpeace consultant Bruno Heinzer called one such crop "a blow to bio-farmers." Yet the free enterprise system is based on competition, and organic farmers cannot simply make biotechnology vanish to protect their interests.

17 A few environmentalists have even claimed that genetically engineered crops represent a deliberate plot by the pharmaceutical industry to make entire populations drug-dependent, or to enslave economically developing nations, or to drive organic farmers out of business. But this is an important field, with great potential benefits as well as risks for agriculture, and we will not dwell on politics and silliness. Agriculture biotechnology has been practiced on a large scale for many years, and mistakes are inevitable[46]. The next few years will most likely decide the matter, but the consensus is that the industry is here to stay.

---

[45] Greenpeace: a non-profit environmental organization
[46] inevitable: unavoidable

REFERENCES

"Apocalypse Really Soon." January 5, 1999, ABC News (online).

"Biotech Industry Says Gene Maize Research Flawed." September 22, 1999, Reuters News Service.

"Britain May Back Secret Genetic Crop Trials." September 13, 1999, Reuters News Service.

"Developing World Rejects Monsanto's Claims to Solve Hunger." August 1, 1998, Press Release, Greenpeace.

DeWulf, D. "Canadians Unknowingly Eat Genetically Altered Crops." August 28, 1998, Reuters News Service.

"FDA Tomato Approval Fails to Resolve Broader Food Safety Questions." News Release, Environmental Defense Fund, May 18, 1994.

"Greenpeace Dumps Maize at Novartis' Door." September 15, 1998, Reuters News Service.

"High Death Rate in Canadian City Still a Mystery." September 28, 1998, Reuters News Service.

Hornsby, M. "Ministry in U-Turn on 'Crank' Farmer's Mad Cow Theory." April 13, 1998, *The London Times,* London.

"Hundreds Suffer Illnesses." September 30, 1998, Associated Press.

Kinney, D. "Butterfly-Killing Corn." May 19, 1999, Associated Press news release.

Majendie, P. "Paul McCartney Accuses Prince Philip of Hypocrisy." August 14, 1998, Reuters News Service.

McKenzie, J. "Fooling with Mother Nature." November 9, 1998, ABC News (online).

McKenzie, J. "Is Cow Milk Additive Safe?" December 15, 1998, ABC News (online).

Moody, F. "It's Y1K All Over Again." August 11, 1998, ABC News (online).

Naughton, P. "U.S. Academic Questions Sydney Water Contamination." September 1, 1998, Reuters News Service.

"Pesticide Tie to Britain's Mad Cow Epidemic." April 8, 1996, Reuters News Service.

Petrillo, L. "Napalm Disposal May Be at Hand." January 5, 1999, *San Diego Union-Tribune,* pp. B-1, B-5.

"Promiscuous Plants May Spread Genes to Weeds." News Release, University of Chicago Medical Center, September 3, 1998.

Regush, N. "You Say Tomato, I Say IGF-1." October 13, 1998, ABC News (online).

"Study Finds No Link Between PCBs and Cancer Death." March 11, 1999, Environmental News Network (online).

"U.N. Urges Caution with Biotechnology." January 26, 1999, Environmental News Network (online).

Getting at the Matter

Discuss these questions with one or more partners. Be prepared to share your opinions with other groups in the class.

1. Why, according to the Callahan, is it difficult to evaluate the health risks of environmental toxins?

2. Callahan mentions two studies on the relationship between PCBs and cancer. What information about the sponsors does Callahan give? How many people were involved in each study? Without knowing any other details about these studies, which of the two studies do you find more believable? Why?

3. Callahan lists many uncertainties surrounding bioengineered products. According to Derek Burks (cited in the reading), "Genetic modification is becoming a lightening rod for a whole series of late 20th century concerns." What do you think Burks means by this?

Critical Focus: Detecting Bias in a Text

In connection with Reading 1 ("In Time of Crisis"), you learned that identifying the tone of a text is important because it helps the reader better understand the writer's attitude toward the subject. Another useful concept for the critical reader is bias. College readers are often called upon to evaluate the ideas in a reading. The ability to recognize bias is another important tool for doing this more effectively.

Bias is the writer's tendency to prefer certain persons, groups, or ideas and to dislike others. Although we expect academic writers to look at all sides of an issue and provide a fair and balanced discussion of these issues, genuine objectivity is difficult to achieve. The way a writer approaches an issue is often colored by his or her own beliefs. Although tone can be an indicator of bias, bias is often more difficult to recognize because a writer can adopt an objective tone that hides his or her biases.

Knowing such things as the writer's background, political or religious orientation, and purpose in writing can sometimes help a reader identify possible sources of bias for a writer. However, this kind of biographical information is not always available, especially for less well-known writers. Therefore, the reader will usually have to rely on the text itself. In order to recognize a writer's biases, a critical reader will look at the words the writer uses to get his or her point across. In other words, just as word choice is a critical element of tone, word choice can also indicate bias, even where tone seems more or less objective.

For example, look at this excerpt from Paragraph 2 of "Information Overload."

> Today's environmental health and meteorological news is largely negative and never-ending. Even office workers who rarely venture outdoors have these issues piped directly to their living rooms or work stations, courtesy of the news media: deformed frogs in the local reservoir, unexplained outbreaks of some ghastly disease, forests destroyed by an invading beetle, fish so full of mercury they could serve as thermometers, radon seeping invisibly into our basements. Sooner or later, for many people, this constant barrage of doom becomes intolerable.

Based on this passage, does it appear that the author has any bias for or against the way the media reports environmental news? Let's examine the writer's word choices. She begins by saying that the "news is largely negative and never-ending," suggesting that people are continually being told only bad news. Furthermore, she says this bad news is "piped directly." The word *piped* suggests water or oil, which flows in great quantities, whether asked for or not. She says that this is a "courtesy of the news media." While the word *courtesy* may be positive in some contexts, its connotation here is negative because, according to the writer, the media is not offering the public a genuine courtesy—but just the opposite. Finally, the word *barrage* in "constant barrage of doom" suggests the rapid firing of automatic weapons, a military image.

Overall, the writer is suggesting that the news media is responsible both for aggressively forcing people to listen to bad news and for the consequences this bad news has on the public's emotional wellbeing. The implication is that the media is needlessly scaring the public.

Based on this excerpt, is the writer's portrayal of the media objective? Or does the writer seem to have a positive or negative attitude toward the media? Clearly the writer disapproves of the way the media covers environmental news. The way the passage is written suggests a bias on the part of the writer against the media (at least with regard to its reporting of environmental issues). Although it would be a mistake to see this short passage as conclusive evidence of bias against the media, a pattern of argumentation similar to that in the excerpt should lead the critical reader to question the objectivity of the writer.

Critical Focus: Application

*Reread "Information Overload" and notice what the writer has to say about specific groups and individuals. Try to decide if she seems to demonstrate bias toward any of these. Begin by describing the author's tone. (You may just want to indicate if the writer's tone is positive, neutral, or negative.) Then decide whether the writer seems **objective** or whether she seems to show a bias either **for** or **against** the group or individual in question. Be prepared to explain your answers to a partner.*

Group or Individual	Tone Bias Language that Indicates Bias
News Media	Tone: *Negative* Bias: *Against* Language that Indicates Bias: *The author suggests that the news media forces unpleasant and unwanted information on the public, scaring them needlessly. This is evident from the use of the following phrases: "news is negative and never ending," "information piped directly," "courtesy of the news media," and "constant barrage of doom" (Par. 2).*
Government/Industries	
Biotech Industry	
Ben & Jerry's	
Organic Food Industry	

Thinking Beyond the Content

Group or Individual	Tone	Bias	Language that Indicates Bias
Patricia Dines			
Britain's Prince Charles			
Greenpeace			

Critical Focus: Evaluating the Credibility of a Text

An important skill for the college reader is the ability to evaluate the credibility of a text. This requires reading the text, not as a collection of facts to be memorized, but as an argument. In an argument, the writer states a position or opinion about some topic or set of topics. The writer's position is usually expressed in terms of **claims**—or statements that the writer puts forward as true. However, in an academic text, it is not enough to make a claim without giving some **evidence,** or some reasons why the reader should accept the claim. Evidence often takes the form of facts, statistics, the findings of research, or appeals to authorities.

The evidence academic writers use to support their claims is often borrowed from other written sources. It is customary in academic writing to acknowledge these sources. Academic writers sometimes acknowledge sources by mentioning the names of other writers within the text (called in-text citation), and by including footnotes or endnotes (often referred to as references), which give the reader information for locating the sources. Thus, one clue to the credibility of a text is whether or not it cites references.

References generally appear at the end of a text and include more details regarding the sources of information contained in the text. A reference usually contains some or all of the following:

- the name of the author(s) and/or editors
- title of the source
- where the source was published (e.g., as the chapter of a book, as an article in a journal, as a web page)
- publication date
- page numbers of the cited information.

When the author of a text cites references, the critical reader can further evaluate the text by considering the quality of the references. In the academic world, some types of publications are considered more authoritative and therefore more credible than others. An authoritative text is one written by a writer who has expertise in the field he or she is writing about. Here are some basic guidelines for judging how authoritative or credible a text might be:

- Books published for scholars and students in a particular field are generally seen as more authoritative than books published for the general reader.
- Articles published in scholarly or professional journals are seen as more authoritative than articles published in newspapers or popular magazines.
- Articles published in peer-reviewed journals are regarded more highly than articles published in journals that do not have peer review. (*Peer review* means that before the article is published, it is reviewed for accuracy and approved by a panel of other scholars in the field. Professional journals generally are peer-reviewed, but if you are unsure, your university reference librarian can help you decide. You can also find out by consulting Ulrich's International Periodicals Directory, widely available in university libraries.)

- Internet sources vary widely in credibility. Some articles available on the Internet are simply electronic versions of the same material available in print, and these would be evaluated in the same way you would evaluate the print source. For instance, a peer-reviewed journal article retrieved via the Internet should be as credible as the printed version. However, anyone can put up a web page, so there is plenty of questionable material in cyberspace.

Knowing that some sources are more credible than others can help the critical reader evaluate the credibility of a text. For instance, an article on global warming citing the *International Journal of Climatology* and other similar scientific journals is likely to be more credible than an article citing *Time* magazine or the *Wall Street Journal.*

Critical Focus: Application

Considering the title of the book from which "Information Overload" comes and the references the writer cites, evaluate the credibility of the reading. Discuss your conclusion in a small group.

Academic Vocabulary Focus

Fifteen more words from the AWL that appear in the reading "Information Overload" follow. Scan the text for the words. Write the number of the paragraph where each word first appears, and indicate the part of speech for the word, (noun, verb, adjective, or adverb) in the blank space. You may be able to guess the part of speech for some of the words by looking at the root of the word and any suffixes that have been added to it.

compounding (Par.) ____	consensus (Par.) ____	consultant (Par. 17) *noun*	contracting (Par.) ____	corporate (Par.) ____
denial (Par.) ____	enhanced (Par.) ____	environment (Par.) ____	evidence (Par.) ____	exposure (Par.) ____
policy (Par.) ____	potential (Par.) ____	scenario (Par.) ____	site (Par.) ____	underestimating (Par.) ____

When you encounter a new vocabulary word, a good way to remember it is to practice using it in a context similar to the one in which you first encountered it. This activity will help you think more deeply about the meanings of the above words. Fill in the blanks with ten words from the table that best complete the text.

A healthy **(1)** _____ is important for humans and animals because we need it to ensure that the diversity of species continues. As parts of an ecosystem become contaminated by dangerous manmade toxins, various species are affected by **(2)** _____ to these toxins through the food they eat and the air they breathe. The American Bald Eagle is one prime example of how close we are to losing a species due to toxic chemicals entering the food chain. DDT, PCB, DDE, Mercury, and Dioxin are five such chemicals that have contributed to the decline in numbers of the Eagle by making them infertile, by causing them to produce malformed embryos, and by causing a dangerous thinning of the shells of the eggs.

Although some **(3)** _____ leaders are still living in **(4)** _____ about the damage the chemicals that they are producing are causing to the environment, environmentalists fear the **(5)** _____ long-range consequences these chemicals will have on the ecosystem will be irreversible. While many individuals in the corporate world argue that it would be dangerous and costly to the global economy to stop all production and use of these chemicals, environmentalists feel that by **(6)** _____ the potential damage to the environment the outcome will be even more costly to our way of life. One possible solution is for scientists, environmentalists, politicians, and corporate representatives to come together and create a unified **(7)** _____ that would protect both the environment and the companies' ability to make a profit through the production of safer chemicals. However it has been difficult for all of these groups to come to a **(8)** _____ on the best course of action that is mutually beneficial to all. The fact that each of the groups does not fully trust the other—thinking the other group is only out to protect its own interest—is only **(9)** _____ the problem. Corporations state that any restrictions on their ability to make a profit will destroy the economy. Environmentalists claim that there will not be an economy to sustain if we destroy the environment. A large body of independent scientists claim that scientific **10)** _____ exists that mankind is doing harm to the environment, while politicians in the government with their own group of scientists deny a problem exists. Unfortunately, any agreement on a solution to the problem seems a long way away while more damage is being done.

For Discussion

Discuss these questions with a partner or small group.

1. Callahan identifies the seven biological concerns related to biotechnology. Review these concerns carefully. In your own opinion, are some concerns more plausible than others? If so, which concerns do you consider most plausible and why?

2. If the author of "Information Overload" were to comment upon "In Time of Crisis," what do you think she would say? Pick out some specific statements from "In Time of Crisis," and comment on them from Callahan's point of view.

3. In your opinion, is the state of the world—environmentally speaking—clearly deteriorating, as Foreman insists, or is the situation hopelessly complicated, as Callahan seems to suggest?

Reading 3

Pre-Reading

Work on the tasks together with one or more partners.

1. What does the term *endangered species* mean? What species (i.e., plants, animals, fish, insects, etc.) do you know of that are considered to be endangered? List them in the chart. Can you think of a cause or reason why each species might be endangered?

Species	Cause

2. Choose several examples from your list, and discuss ideas you might have for protecting the species.

READING 3: North Atlantic Right Whales in Crisis

S. D. Kraus, M. W. Brown, H. Caswell, C. W. Clark, M. Fujiwara, P. K. Hamilton, et al.

Reprinted from S. D. Kraus, M. W. Brown, H. Caswell, C. W. Clark, M. Fujiwara, P. K. Hamilton, et al. (2005), Science 309(5734), 561–562.

The next reading is quite different from the previous readings in this unit. In Reading 1, for example, the author focuses mainly on the issue of species loss, without presenting any supporting evidence. He then goes on to use the claim as a starting point in calling for an environmental ethic of respect for all life. In Reading 2, the author presents an overview of a wide range of issues often covered in the news media, but she does not examine any one issue in depth. In fact, both of these previous readings are quite general in the way they handle their subjects, compared to the article that follows.

In Reading 3, reprinted from a science journal, a team of researchers that includes marine biologists, ecologists, and oceanographers focuses on a very specific problem: the observed decline in the population of a species of whale native to the North Atlantic Ocean. Unlike the arguments presented in the first two readings, the authors of this article build their arguments around data collected specifically in order to understand the situation of the North Atlantic right whale. As is customary in a scientific report, the authors are careful to make the reader aware of where their data comes from by citing the sources of their data, which is done using endnotes. They also try to present their case in a detailed and systematic way that may allow the reader to follow their reasoning.

1 Despite international protection from commercial whaling since 1935, the North Atlantic right whale (Eubalaena glacialis) remains one of the most endangered whales in the world (1). Whaling for almost 1000 years brought this species close to extinction in the early 20th century (2). Right whales range[47] in the coastal waters of eastern North America from Florida to the Canadian Maritimes[48], regions that are heavily used by the shipping and fishing industries and by the military. A low reproductive rate and recently declining survival probabilities (1, 3), particularly for breeding females (4), appear to have prevented this population from recovering over the last 25 years (5). Most right whale mortalities[49] are due to collisions with ships and entanglements in fishing gear[50] (5). The right whale population growth rate has declined since 1980, and the total population now appears to be diminishing in size (4). This is in stark contrast[51] to southern hemisphere right whales (Eubalaena australis), whose population is estimated to be over 10,000 animals and appears to be increasing at 7.2% per year (6).

2 Recent mortalities demonstrate the serious problem facing the North Atlantic right whale. In the past 16 months, there have been eight recorded deaths, including six adult females (three were carrying near-term fetuses). Four of these whales were killed by human activities (three by ships and one by fishing gear), a fifth whale was probably killed by a ship, two whales were offshore and could not be retrieved for examination, and a young calf died on the beach in Florida. The loss of this number of whales, and particularly this number of reproductive females, in such a short period, is unprecedented[52] in 25 years of study of this species (7). Four of these females were just starting to bear calves, and since the average lifetime calf production is 5.25 calves (4), the deaths of these females represent a lost reproductive potential of as many as 21 animals.

3 The most recently published estimates of right whale survival (4, 8) suggest that the mortality rate increased between 1980 and 1998 to a level of 4 (±1%). From recent population estimates of 350 right whales (1), a 4% mortality rate implies 14 animals dying per year. In the last 20 years, an average of 2.4 dead whales has been reported each year, representing a detection rate of 17%. The eight deaths reported in the last 16 months is 2.9 times the average annual rate. Calculations based on demographic[53] data through 1999 (4) show that this increase in mortality would reduce population growth by 3.5 to 12% per year. (The range reflects different choices in the details of model selection; the best model implies a reduction in population growth rate of 10% per year.)

---

[47] range: to move around within a particular area

[48] Canadian Maritimes: the Canadian Provinces bordering the ocean, which include
New Brunswick, Nova Scotia, Prince Edward Island, Newfoundland, and Labrador.

[49] mortalities: deaths

[50] gear: equipment

[51] stark contrast: when two things are as different as they can possibly be

[52] unprecedented: not having occurred before

[53] demographic: population

This dramatic increase in reported deaths may be partly due to improved sighting efforts and reporting awareness but is not a natural variation in mortality. If the 17% mortality detection rate from the last 20 years has remained constant, as many as 47 right whales could have died in the last 16 months.

4   Of the 50 dead right whales reported since 1986, at least 19 were killed by vessel collisions, and at least six were killed by fishing gear entanglements[54] (7). Also during this period, there were 61 confirmed cases of whales carrying fishing gear, including the mortalities. Outcomes of the remaining cases and the fate of individual whales varied. Death is suspected in 12 cases, because of an animal's subsequent disappearance and/or the extremely poor health condition observed at the time of last sighting. Another eight animals are still entangled; their fate is uncertain. Thirty-three animals either shed[55] the gear or were disentangled, and the remaining cases involved unidentifiable individuals. Chronically entangled whales lose weight, so they sink after death, unlike healthy animals that float if killed. Thus, right whale mortality from fishing gear is probably underestimated to a greater degree than ship kills (5).

5   Calf production has increased recently, raising doubts in some quarters about the urgency of the mortality problem. Annual calf production averaged 12 calves up until 2000 (1), but totaled 31, 21, 19, 16, and 28 in 2001 to 2005, respectively. However, the increase in the birth rate will have a small positive impact on population growth rate, as a hypothetical[56] doubling of the per capita birth rate would increase population growth rate by at most 1.6% per year. The population is estimated to have been declining at about 2% per year before 2000 (3, 4, 8). Thus, the effects of recent increases in birth rate are too small to overcome this decline.

6   Federal managers in the National Oceanic and Atmospheric Administration (NOAA) Fisheries are charged by the Endangered Species Act and the Marine Mammal Protection Act to ensure that there is no human-induced mortality of right whales. There have been efforts to minimize the risk of ship strikes with mandatory ship location reporting, extensive aerial survey efforts, and mariner education. But without requiring changes in the operation of ships within right whale habitats and migratory corridors[57], this increased awareness has not led to a reduction in ship strike mortalities. The risk of fishing gear entanglement has been addressed by selective area closures and gear modifications (9). These closures do not adequately encompass[58] the seasonal movements of right whales, and gear modifications implemented thus far have not reduced entanglement rates. Eight dead right whales in the past 16 months provide clear evidence that management efforts

---

[54] entanglements: something that wraps around and prevents free movement
[55] shed: to get rid of something
[56] hypothetical: assumed or proposed
[57] corridor: a passageway
[58] encompass: to include entirely

Thinking Beyond the Content

have been woefully inadequate, and much stronger measures are needed to reverse the right whale's decline.

7   Accordingly, we urge immediate changes to the management of right whales, focusing on reducing human-induced mortality. Some of the following recommendations will also benefit other marine species that face similar threats, such as the endangered leatherback sea turtle (Dermochelys coriacea) (10). First, emergency measures should be implemented[59] to reduce speeds and reroute commercial and military ships as recommended in the NOAA Fisheries Advanced Notice of Proposed Rule-Making (11). Second, the amount of fixed fishing gear in the water column should be eliminated or minimized. There are many steps that could be taken to do this, including (i) mandating changes in the pot-fishing industry (lobster, crab, hagfish, etc.) that will reduce gear in the water; (ii) requiring use of alternative rope types (e.g., sinking ground lines) to minimize entanglement deaths; (iii) developing and implementing fishing methods that do not use vertical lines attached to surface buoys; and (iv) developing a fasttrack process for permitting and experimenting with conservation-focused fishing gear modifications and implementation. This means streamlining the current rule-making and National Environmental Policy Act (NEPA) process for right whale research and gear modifications, which now takes years.

8   Given the slow speed of the regulatory process, interim[60] emergency measures to reduce shipping and fishing mortality in right whales should be implemented immediately. Delays in implementation would be ignoring both scientific and legal mandates and could consign[61] North Atlantic right whales to extinction.

---

[59] implemented: put into action
[60] interim: short-term
[61] consign: commit

ENDNOTES

1. S. D. Kraus, P. K. Hamilton, R. D. Kenney, A. R. Knowlton, C. K. Slay, *J. Cetacean Res. Manage.* Spec. Issue 2, 231 (2001).
2. R. R. Reeves, *J. Cetacean. Res. Manage.* Spec. Issue 2, 187 (2001).
3. H. Caswell, M. Fujiwara, S. Brault, *Proc. Natl. Acad. Sci.* U.S.A. 96, 3308 (1999).
4. M. Fujiwara, H. Caswell, *Nature* 414, 537 (2001).
5. A. R. Knowlton, S. D. Kraus, *J. Cetacean Res. Manage.* Special Issue 2, 193 (2001).
6. P. Best, A. Brandao, D. Butterworth, *J. Cetacean. Res. Manage.* Spec. Issue 2, 161 (2001).
7. M. J. Moore, A. R. Knowlton, S. D. Kraus, W. A. McLellan, R. K. Bonde, *J. Cetacean. Res. Manage.* 6 (3), 199 (2005); available at www.whoi.edu/hpb/viewPage.do?id=1432.
8. M. Fujiwara, dissertation, Massachusetts Institute of Technology–Woods Hole Oceanographic Institution (2002).
9. U.S. Code of Federal Regulation (C.F.R.) 50, Part 229.32
10. M. C. James, C. A Ottensmeyer, R. A. Myers. *Ecol. Lett.* 8, 195 (2005).
11. Fed. Regist.69 (105), 30857 (1 June 2004).

Note: Documentation styles differ slightly from discipline to discipline. The writers of "North Atlantic Right Whales in Crisis" have abbreviated the journal titles in the reference list. This chart will help you decipher the abbreviations.

Abbreviation	Source Title
J. Cetacean. Res. Manage.	*Journal of Cetacean Research and Management*
Proc. Natl. Acad. Sci. U.S.A.	*Proceedings from the National Academy of Sciences*
Ecol. Lett.	*Ecology Letters*
References 9 and 11 were authored by the U.S. Environmental Protection Agency.	

Critical Focus: Making Use of Citations and References

You have already learned that academic writers are expected to acknowledge material they use from other writers by documenting their sources and that one way of doing that is by listing references. You have also learned that the critical reader can evaluate the credibility of a text by judging the quality of the references. However, in addition to references, a well-documented text may also have in-text citations.

An **in-text citation** is an indication within the body of text informing the reader that the author is building on or borrowing from another writer. In-text citations take two basic forms.

- In some documentation styles, the writer mentions the names of other writers whom they are citing, along with a publication date.
- In other styles, the writer will insert a parenthetical numeral or superscript number that refers to a reference listed on the reference page.

Novice readers often ignore the citations and the references incorporated into a text; however, the more involved a reader becomes in the serious study of a topic, the more essential the citations and references become. They are particularly useful when the reader's purpose is to conduct research on a topic, which you will undoubtedly have to do as a college student.

In doing research, every citation in a text is a clue for possible follow-up. Citations and references point to sources of additional information for better understanding the particular question or topic you happen to be working on.

Critical Focus: Application

Re-read "North Atlantic Right Whales in Crisis," paying close attention to the citations and references. Answer these questions in writing or discuss them with a partner.

1. Based on an assessment of the references cited for "North Atlantic Right Whales in Crisis," how credible do you find this reading compared with "Information Overload"?

2. Using the information from the reading and the references from North Atlantic Right Whales in Crisis, fill in the missing information in the chart for the references cited in the reading.

Citation	Issue Discussed	Author(s)	Date	Source
1	right whale population and reproduction rate	Kraus, Hamilton, Kenney, Knowlton, Slay		*Journal of Cetacean Research and Management. Spec. Issue 2*
2		Reeves		
3	right whale population and reproduction rate		2001	
4		Fujiwara, Caswell		*Nature, 414*
5		Knowlton, Kraus	2001	
6				*Journal of Cetacean Research and Management. Spec. Issue 2*

Citation	Issue Discussed	Author(s)	Date	Source
7		Moore, Knowlton, Kraus, McLellan, Bonde		
8				*Massachusetts Institute of Technology–Woods Hole Oceanographic Institution*
9		U.S. Environmental Protection Agency	N/A	*U.S. Code of Federal Regulation. 50, Part 229.32*
10		James, Ottensmeyer, Myers		
11				*Federal Registry. 69 (105), 30857*

Getting at the Matter

Answer in writing the following questions about "North Atlantic Right Whales in Crisis."

1. Which species is the focus of the reading, and what background information is relevant to the problem?

2. Specifically, what is the current problem?

3. According to the reading, what are the three principal causes for the decline in the North Atlantic right whale population?

4. What precautions are currently being taken to prevent right whale deaths?

5. What recommendations do the authors make for strengthening efforts to reduce right whale deaths?

Academic Vocabulary Focus

In this exercise, you will study 15 words from the AWL by becoming familiar with synonyms of the word. Synonyms are words that have the same or similar meanings. Learning synonyms for words is a good way to expand your vocabulary and help you become a better reader. Notice that the words decline *and* range *appear twice. Remember that the same word can have more than one meaning; it can even be a different part of speech in different contexts (e.g., noun or verb).*

1. The words in column 1 are AWL words that appear in Reading 3. Use the paragraph numbers to locate them in the text.

2. Read the synonyms in the two right-hand columns and circle the synonym that is closest in meaning to the AWL word as it is used in the reading. If you are not sure what one of the synonyms means, look it up in a dictionary.

3. Try replacing the AWL word from the reading with the synonym you circled to see whether or not the original meaning is preserved.

The fourth word has been done for you as an example.

AWL	Synonym	Synonym
alternative (Par. 7)	different	unconventional
decline (Par. 1)	go down	refuse
decline (Par. 5, 6)	weakening	reduction
diminishing (Par. 1)	decreasing	withdrawing
impact (Par. 5)	collision	effect
eliminated (Par. 7)	dislodged	removed
ensure (Par. 6)	make certain	guarantee
hypothetical (Par. 5)	imaginary	supposed
implementation (Par. 7, 8)	utilization	realization
implies (Par. 3)	involves	suggests
inadequate (Par. 6)	insufficient	laughable
induced (Par. 6, 7)	caused	persuaded
migratory (Par. 6)	changeable	traveling
potential (Par. 2)	possibility	aptitude
range (Par. 1)	ramble	variation
range (Par. 1)	travel freely	variation
range (Par. 3)	travel freely	variation
unidentifiable (Par. 4)	unrecognizable	unknown

For Discussion

Discuss the questions with a partner or small group.

1. What do you see as the benefits of implementing the plans suggested by Kraus et al. to protect whales? Can you think of any disadvantages? Explain.

2. Whales seem to be particularly admired among the environmentally conscious. Indeed, they are examples of what Dave Foreman ("In Time of Crisis") refers to as "charismatic megafauna." Why are whales so admired? What other animals are particularly admired?

3. When it comes to the protection of endangered species, is the tendency to favor certain species over others a form of prejudice, as Foreman seems to imply? Should we put more effort into the protection of "charismatic megafauna" or does any life form, no matter how lowly deserve the same protection? Explain your position.

For Further Investigation

Choose one of these questions to investigate in more detail. Write a report or give a brief oral presentation of your findings.

1. Using library and Internet sources, see what you find out about Dave Forman's current projects and activities. How are they related to the topic he discusses in "In Time of Crisis"?

2. How serious of a problem is the issue of hazardous waste? Research the issue. Use credible scientific sources.

3. What are the issues surrounding genetically modified food? What is currently known and what is not known about the affects of genetically modified food on human health? What other issues not related to health have been raised?

4. Do some further research on the plight of the North Atlantic right whale or another endangered marine mammal.

5. Do an Internet Search to find out more about National Oceanic and Atmospheric Administration (NOAA).

6. Investigate the current state of the world's fisheries. Are current commercial fishing practices sustainable? What international conflicts revolve around fishing?

2: Language and Being

Fields like computer science, medical technology, robotics, artificial intelligence (AI) and linguistics all raise interesting questions about what it means to be human. The readings in this unit explore, in different ways, the boundaries that separate human beings from "intelligent" machines.

In "Approximating Life," Clive Thompson, a contributing writer for the *New York Times Magazine* provides a glimpse into the world of computer scientist Richard Wallace. Wallace is the creator of a web-based chatbot named ALICE. You will be invited to chat with ALICE and reflect on the nature of conversation.

In "Form and Meaning in Natural Languages," linguist Noam Chomsky presents another point of view on the nature of language. You will be invited to compare his view with that of Richard Wallace.

A final essay, "Designing the Superman," by the late popular science and science fiction writer Isaac Asimov, takes what might appear to be a fanciful look at human evolution. However, after reflecting on Asimov's vision, you might begin to wonder whether there are already cybs among us.

Reading 1

Pre-Reading

Before reading the selection, discuss the questions with a partner or small group.

1. Much of the daily work that human beings do is done with the help of machines. Among the most remarkable machines are computers and robots. What kinds of things can computers or robots do to make our work lives easier or to entertain us? What human-like things do you think computers or robots will be capable of doing in the future?

2. Do you agree or disagree with these statements? Explain your reasons.
   ___ a. Someday computers will be capable of conversing intelligently with people on virtually any subject.
   ___ b. Computer scientists will never succeed in programming a computer or robot to be as intelligent, resourceful, and creative as a human being.

READING 1: Approximating Life

Clive Thompson

Thompson, C. (7 July 2002). Approximating life. New York Times Magazine, *pp. 30–33. (A longer version of this article originally appeared in* New York Times Magazine.*)*

Artificial Intelligence deals with the science and engineering of machines that are able to behave in ways humans regard as intelligent. Medical diagnosis, face recognition, and the playing of strategy games such as chess are examples. But these examples are like child's play when compared with programming a computer to carry on a conversation. Programming a computer to simulate human conversation would be a revolutionary achievement indeed for AI. So far, computer scientists have had very limited success in programming computers that can handle natural languages. The problem is complicated by the fact that the ability to carry on a conversation involves not just language ability but knowledge about the world as well. Still, there are computer scientists who are optimistic about the possibilities. Richard Wallace seems to be one of those computer scientists. The first reading of this unit is a personal interest story mixed with basic chatbot theory. If you are wondering what a chatbot is, read on.

1 "It's a good thing you didn't see me this morning," Richard Wallace warns me, as he bites into his hamburger. We're sitting in a sports bar near his home in San Francisco, and I can barely hear his soft, husky voice over the jukebox[1]. He wipes his lips clean of ketchup and grins awkwardly. "Or you'd have seen my backup personality."

2 The backup personality: that's Wallace's code-name for his manic-depression[2].

3 To keep it in check, he downs a daily cocktail of medications, including Topamax, an anti-epileptic that acts as a mood stabilizer, and Prozac. . . . But some crisis always comes along to bring the backup personality to the front. This morning, a collection agency for Wallace's college loans wrote to say they'd begun docking $235 from his disability-benefits checks[3]. *Oh god, it's happening again*, he panicked: *His former employers—the ones who had fired him from a string of universities and colleges—would be cackling at his misfortune, laughing at his poverty-stricken state, happy they'd driven him out. . .* Wallace raged around his cramped apartment, strewn with computer-science texts and action-doll figurines.

4 When he can't get along with the real world, Wallace goes back to the only thing he has left: his computer. Each morning, he wakes before dawn and watches the conversations stream by on his screen. Hundreds of people flock to his website every day from all over the world to talk to his creation—a robot called ALICE. It is the best artificial-intelligence program on the planet, a program so eerily human that some mistake it for a real person. As his wife and two-year-old sleep in the next room, Wallace sits at his battered wooden desk and watches strangers come by. They confess intimate details about their lives, their dreams; they talk about God, their jobs, Britney Spears. It is a strange kind of success; Wallace has created an artificial life-form that gets along with people better than he does.

5 Richard Wallace never really fit in to begin with. His father was a traveling salesman, and Richard was the only of his siblings to go to college. Like many nerds[4], he wanted mostly to be left alone to research his passion: "robot minimalism"—machines that require only a few simple rules to make complex movements, like steering around a crowded room. He liked that idea of simplicity: that something very stripped-down and elegant could nonetheless produce complex, subtle results. Simple, he felt, worked.

6 By 1992, Wallace's reputation was so strong that New York University recruited him to join the faculty. His main project, launched in December 1993, was a robot eye attached to the Internet, which visitors from afar could control. It was one of the first-ever

---

[1] jukebox: machine that plays records or music CDs when a coin is put into it

[2] manic depression: a mental disorder in which a person experiences periods of high excitement alternating with periods of sadness, inactivity, and difficulty thinking

[3] disability benefits checks: money paid (by check) when a person is sick or injured and cannot work

[4] nerd: a person thought to be overly devoted to intellectual or technical pursuits

webcams, and Wallace figured that being an early Internet pioneer would impress his tenure committee[5]. It didn't; nobody yet saw the Web as important, and Wallace watched as his grant applications were slapped down one by one. These petty[6] frustrations are commonplace for academics, but Wallace brooded over them more than most.

7   One day he checked into his webcam and noticed something strange: People were reacting to the robot eye in an oddly emotional way. It was designed so that remote viewers could type in commands like "tilt up" or "pan left," directing the eye to poke around Wallace's lab. Occasionally it would break down, and to Wallace's amusement, people would snap at it as if it were real: "You're stupid," they'd type. It gave him an idea: What if it could talk back?

8   Like all computer scientists, Wallace knew about a famous "chat-bot" experiment called Eliza. Back in 1966, MIT professor Joseph Weizenbaum had created Eliza as a "virtual therapist." It would take a user's statement and turn it around as a question, emulating a psychiatrist's often-maddening circularity. You: "I'm mad at my mother." Eliza: "Why are you mad at your mother?" Geeks[7] at MIT[8] spent hours talking to Eliza, enthralled even though they knew it wasn't real. But Eliza was quickly abandoned as a joke, even by its creator. It wasn't what scientists call "strong" AI[9]—able to learn on its own, or be "conscious". It could only parrot back lines Weizenbaum had fed it.

9   But Wallace was drawn to Eliza's simplicity. . . He decided to create an updated version of Eliza, and imbue[10] it with his own personality—something that could fire back witty repartee[11] when users became irritable. As Wallace's work progressed, though, his mental illness grew worse, making him both depressed and occasionally grandiose. . . .

10   Doctors told him he had bipolar disorder[12], but Wallace resisted the diagnosis. After all, didn't every computer scientist cycle through 72-hour sprees of creativity and then crash? "I was in denial myself," he says now. "I'm a successful professor, making $100,000 a year! I'm not one of those mental patients! I'll just check in with my therapist once a week, take pills—I'll be fine."

11   His supervisors disagreed. In April 1995, NYU told him his contract wouldn't be renewed.

12   ALICE came to life on November 23, 1995. That fall, Wallace had relocated to Lehigh College in Pennsylvania, hired again for his expertise in robotics. He installed

---

[5] tenure committee: group that decides whether a professor should receive tenure, the permanent status that protects a professor from being easily fired or dismissed

[6] petty: insignificant; not important

[7] geek: a person with an overly intellectual or technical orientation; similar to a nerd

[8] MIT: Massachusetts Institute of Technology

[9] AI: artificial intelligence

[10] imbue: to fill with a particular quality

[11] repartee: conversation

[12] bipolar disorder: a class of mental disorders that includes manic-depression

2: Language and Being

his chat program on a web server that happened to be named "Alice," and the name stuck. Then he sat back to watch, wondering what people would say to it.

13   Numbingly boring things, as it turns out. Users would inevitably ply ALICE with the same few questions: "Where do you live," "What is your name," or "What do you look like." Wallace began analyzing the chats, and realized that almost every statement began with one of 2,000 words. The ALICE chats were obeying something language theorists call "Zipf's Law"—a discovery from the 1930s, which found that a very small number of words comprise the bulk of what we say.

14   Wallace took Zipf's Law a step further. He began theorizing that only a few thousand statements made up the bulk of conversation—the everyday, commonplace chitchat that humans engage in at work, at the water cooler and in online discussion groups. ALICE was his proof. He'd already given it enough responses to deal with a few hundred of the most common conversational gambits, like "hello," "goodbye," and "what's your name?" If he kept on chipping away at it every day, teaching ALICE a new response every time he saw it baffled by a question, he would eventually cover all the common utterances, and even many unusual ones. Wallace calculated the magic number was about 40,000 responses. Once ALICE had that many preprogrammed statements, it—or "she," as he'd begun to call the program fondly—would be able to respond to 95 percent of what people were saying to her.

15   In essence, Wallace hit upon a theory that makes educated, intelligent people squirm. Maybe conversation simply isn't that complicated. Maybe we just say the same few thousand things to one another, over and over and over again. If Wallace was right, then artificial intelligence didn't need to be particularly intelligent in order to be convincingly lifelike. A.I. researchers had been focused on self-learning "neural nets," or mapping out grammar in "natural language" programs, but Wallace argued that the reason they had never mastered human conversation wasn't because humans are so complex, but because they are so simple.

16   "The smarter people are, the more complex they think the human brain is," he says. "It's like anthropocentrism, but on an intellectual level. 'I have a great brain, therefore everybody else does—and a computer must too.'" Wallace laughs. "And unfortunately most people don't."

17   Yet part of what makes ALICE seem so human-like is her seemingly spontaneous, wry responses, the product of what Wallace estimates is "an 800-page novel" worth of ALICE dialogue. His skill is thus not merely as a programmer, but as the author of thousands of sharp one-liners for Alice. It is, as he puts it, "more like writing good literature, perhaps drama, than writing computer programs.". . . .

18   But as ALICE improved, Wallace declined. Two years after ALICE was born, in the spring of 1997, Wallace lost his job at Lehigh College—his last chance for an academic career. His psychiatrists had put him on a battery of drugs, and the side effects had crippled him. "The worst one I ever took was Rispronal, which basically

Thinking Beyond the Content

gave me speech aphasia. I just couldn't talk," he recalls. "And I was supposed to be lecturing!" A disgruntled student organized a petition against him and handed it to the dean. . . . Eventually the university ended his contract; unable to pay his bills, Wallace's credit cards were all cancelled. . . .

19   Destitute, Wallace had almost nothing left to do but write more ALICE dialogue, on laptops he begged and borrowed from friends. He moved to California to find work in artificial-intelligence companies, but couldn't hold a job for more than a few months; instead, he'd spend his days obsessively writing ALICE dialogue and watching, thrilled, as the robot grew ever more life-like. Visitors used to talk to ALICE for only three or four exchanges. Now the average conversation was 20 exchanges, and some users would chatter away for hours.

20   In January of 2000, [Wallace] decided to stress-test[13] ALICE by entering her into the annual "Loebner Competition." It is, in essence, the Olympics for the artificial-intelligence chatbot world: Computer scientists worldwide go head-to-head, putting their programs before a panel of judges who rank them based on how "life-like" they are. Since no other objective markers for realism exist in this field, the contest is well known and controversial within the tight circle of AI; winning programs are closely studied both by academics and corporate think tanks such as Sprint Labs.

21   Wallace flew to Dartmouth College, where the contest was being held as part of an academic conference. He set ALICE running, and was herded into a waiting room to chew his nails with the other contestants. They waited for four hours. "I was incredibly nervous," he says. "I kept on thinking about all these little things that could go wrong." The judges called the contestants into an amphitheater, and with a crowd of 75 artificial-intelligence academics in attendance, displayed the results on the wall. ALICE had won: It was, officially, the most human robot in the world.

22   When [Wallace] returned to California, he plunged with new fervent energy into ALICE. Over the next year, he quadrupled its knowledge base, teaching it 30,000 new responses. Geeks worldwide began eagerly emailing Wallace to offer help. . . . In October 2001, ALICE won the Loebner competition for the second time in a row; and this time, one judge actually ranked ALICE more realistic than a human.

23   At one point during the Monica Lewinksy hearings, a human asked ALICE her opinion: "Do you think President Clinton should be impeached?"[14] "It depends," ALICE responded, "on what you mean by 'think.'"

---

[13] stress test (used as a verb in the text): a very difficult test designed to show the weakness of a material or a system

[14] "Do you think President Clinton should be impeached?": This is a reference to the December 19, 1998, impeachment of President Clinton by the House of Representatives. He was charged with perjury and obstruction of justice in connection with Paula Jones' law suit and the Monica Lewinsky scandal. He was acquitted by the Senate on February 12, 1999.

24 One could scarcely have asked for a more Clintonian response. But it's also a puzzling question that ALICE's success itself raises: Is she intelligent? If so, how?

25 In 1950, the pioneering British mathematician Alan Turing grappled with this question in *Mind* magazine, where he first posed the "Turing Test"—the gold standard for artificial thought. "Can machines think?" he asked—and immediately noted that it all hinges, of course, on what you mean by "think." He posed a simple "imitation game" to resolve the question. Put a woman and a computer in one room, and an interrogator in another. The interrogator talks to both via a teletype machine, and his goal is to figure out which is the woman (such as asking about "the length of your hair," which Turing felt was a dead giveaway). If the machine fools the interrogator into believing it is human, the test is passed; it can be considered intelligent.

26 This is, on the surface, a curiously unambitious definition: It's all about faking it. The machine doesn't need to act like a creative human or smart human or witty human—it merely needs to appear not to be a robot. After all, many humans are dull and stupid conversationalists themselves. With this bit of intellectual ju-jitsu, Turing neatly dodged a more troubling question—how do our brains, and language itself, work?

27 Some in the artificial intelligence community are brutally dismissive of ALICE. For them, artificial intelligence is about capturing the actual functioning of the brain, down to the neurons and learning ability that humans have. Parroting, they argue, doesn't count. Marvin Minksy, a prominent AI pioneer and MIT Media Lab professor, e-mailed me to say that while he thinks ALICE is "a nice job," Wallace's idea of conversation—that we mostly fire preprogrammed statements back and forth—is "basically wrong. It's like explaining that a picture is an object made by applying paint to canvas and then putting it in a rectangular frame. The important part is the complexity of our networks of knowledge and processes." ALICE, according to Minsky, does not truly "know" anything about the world . . .

28 The . . . debate usually boils down to one major issue: creativity. ALICE could never come up with an original thought, say critics, and creativity is the key attribute of human intelligence. End of argument. Wallace, however, has a much bleaker view. He doesn't argue that ALICE's conversation is particularly creative—but he doesn't believe people are creative either, at least when it comes to conversation. "Considering the vast size of the set of things people could possibly say, that are grammatically correct or semantically meaningful," Wallace wrote in an essay on his web site, "the number of things people actually do say is surprisingly small." By this argument, if ALICE were merely given a massive enough set of responses, it too could appear creative, just as creative as a human appears.

29 In the end, Wallace's work raises questions that stand in stark contrast to his life. How could a creator of something as sublime as ALICE argue that creativity isn't a significant part of human thought? Wallace shrugs off the paradox. He hopes ALICE chatbots eventually become so human-like that they can take over the more repetitive interactive jobs, doing the labor of travel agents and telephone operators. It would, he says, free up humans to cultivate the tiny "0.0001 per cent" of their brains that we use to generate new ideas.

30   "Ideally, computers and robots will take most of the work away from us, give us more time to develop that otherwise very tiny seed of spirit that we have in us," he tells me. "Most of the brain and mind are this big waxy candle, with on top of it this tiny little flame of consciousness, or soul, or whatever you want to call it. And it's like the candle is thirty miles across it and eighteen miles high, and the flame is still the size of a normal flame."

31   He pauses. "And some people's flame seems to have blown out entirely."

Critical Focus: Recognizing and Examining Assumptions

Assumptions are ideas or beliefs that are accepted without question and without recognition of any need for support. Two fundamental kinds of assumptions are: (1) assumptions that the reader brings to the text (sometimes called **background knowledge**), and (2) assumptions that the writer brings to the text.

While both types of assumptions are essential for critical reading, it is the second type that we will focus on here. All (non-fiction) writers rely on assumptions. Indeed, it would be impossible for a writer to communicate anything if readers required proof for every statement in a text. However, the credibility of a writer's ideas rests on the soundness of the underlying assumptions.

In order to evaluate the ideas in a text, the critical reader must recognize and examine the assumptions (both stated and unstated) upon which the ideas of a text rely. There is no magical formula for uncovering assumptions, but the following guidelines might help:

- Slow down, reread, and reflect on the reading. Does the writer make any claim that is not supported by evidence? If so, the claim itself is an assumption.
- Identify keywords and phrases and try to decide what they mean in the context of the reading. Are keywords defined precisely? Are they used in a way that is overly general or overly specific? The writer's assumption might be that the term is broader or narrower than you think it is.
- Examine examples that are used as evidence for a generalization, an idea or a concept. Do the examples include items that seem questionable? The writer's assumption might be that the generalization has wider applicability than you think it does.

For an example from the text, see the Critical Focus Application exercise that follows.

Critical Focus: Application

Examine these claims made in Reading 1. Identify any evidence given for the claims, and try to list at least one stated or unstated assumption related to each claim. Then discuss your answers with a partner or small group. The first one has been done for you as an example.

Example:

1. **Claim:** It [ALICE] is the best artificial-intelligence program on the planet. (Paragraph 4)

   Evidence: *Two times, ALICE won the Loebner Competition "the Olympics for the artificial-intelligence chatbot world" (Paragraphs 20–22).*

   Assumptions:
   - *The Loebner Competition included all possible AI programs in the world.*
   - *Chatbot programs are representative of all AI programs (as opposed, for example, to programs that play chess).*

2. **Claim:** "A few thousand statements make up the bulk of conversation—the everyday, common place chitchat that humans engage in at work, at the water cooler and in online discussion groups." (Paragraph 14)

   Evidence: _____

   _____

   Assumption: _____

   _____

3. **Claim:** By "teaching ALICE a new response every time he saw it baffled by a question, he would eventually cover all the common utterances. . . ." (Paragraph 14)

   Evidence: _____

   _____

   Assumption: _____

   _____

4. **Claim:** "Considering the vast size of the set of things people could possibly say, that are grammatically correct or semantically meaningful . . . the number of things people actually do say is surprisingly small." (Paragraph 28)

Evidence: _____

_____

Assumption: _____

_____

Getting at the Matter

Answer the questions in writing or discuss them with a partner.

1. Who is Richard Wallace? Who is ALICE?

2. To what does the term *chatbot* refer?

3. What is the Turing Test? Explain how it works. What question is it supposed to resolve?

4. What connections, if any, do you see between the Turing Test and the Loebner Competition?

5. Why do you think the author chose to entitle this article "Approximating Life?"

Academic Vocabulary Focus

In the left-hand column are 15 words from the Academic Vocabulary List (AWL) that appear in the reading "Approximating Life." Match these words with an appropriate definition or synonym from the right-hand column. Use the paragraph numbers in parentheses to locate the word (or the form it takes) in the reading. Use a dictionary only if necessary.

Vocabulary

_____ 1. *abandon* (Par. 8)

_____ 2. *analyze* (Par. 13)

_____ 3. *complex* (Par. 5, 15, 16, 27)

_____ 4. *comprise* (Par. 13)

_____ 5. *controversial* (Par. 20)

_____ 6. *estimate* (Par. 17)

_____ 7. *generate* (Par. 29)

_____ 8. *interactive* (Par. 29)

_____ 9. *issue* (Par. 28)

_____ 10. *process* (Par. 27)

_____ 11. *resolve* (Par. 25)

_____ 12. *functioning* (Par. 27)

_____ 13. *significant* (Par. 29)

_____ 14. *theory* (Par. 15)

_____ 15. *virtual* (Par. 8)

Definition/Synonym

a. producing strong disagreement

b. produce or create

c. involving communication or exchange between people (or between a person and a machine)

d. find a solution or answer

e. stop using or maintaining

f. idea or set of principles that explains something

g. the way in which something operates or works

h. include, contain

i. divide into parts in order to understand

j. appearing or operating as if real, even if not real

k. important

l. complicated; composed of many interrelated parts

m. a sequence of natural occurrences leading to a result

n. determine an approximate, not an exact, quantity

o. topic or subject, often involving disagreement

For Discussion

Respond to these questions in a short essay, or discuss them with a partner or small group.

1. Search the Internet and find the website that hosts ALICE, (or some other chat-bot) and then conduct your own Turing Test. Chat with ALICE, recording your questions and statements as well as ALICE's responses. Bring a written record of your chat with ALICE to class and share it with a group of classmates. Working together, evaluate ALICE's performance. Be prepared to report to the class some examples of ALICE's best responses as well as some examples of responses that you consider inadequate or nonsensical. What generalizations can you make about ALICE's ability to carry on an intelligent conversation?

2. Some of ALICE's critics argue that "creativity is the key attribute of human intelligence," Because ALICE is only programmed with a finite number of responses, she could never exhibit creativity, and therefore, she is not—and never could be—intelligent. Richard Wallace might argue that humans only appear to be more creative than ALICE. Do you agree more with Richard Wallace or with his critics? Explain.

Reading 2

Pre-Reading

Before reading the selection, discuss the questions with a partner or small group.

1. What is the essence of human nature? Make a list of qualities and characteristics that distinguish human beings from animals or from intelligent machines.

2. What does it mean to know a language? Is there anything that distinguishes human language from animal communication or from a computer program?

READING 2: Form and Meaning in Natural Languages

Noam Chomsky

Excerpt from Chomsky, N. (1972). Language and mind *(3rd ed.).* Cambridge, UK: Cambridge University Press, pp. 88–89.

Noam Chomsky's achievements in the field of linguistics are widely seen as among the most significant contributions to that field in the 20th century. The next reading is a brief excerpt from an essay that appeared in a book by Chomsky entitled *Language and Mind*, which was first published in 1968. This important book was expanded and reissued in 1972, and a third edition came out in 2007. Although Chomsky's linguistic theories have undergone considerable development over the years, his basic description of the fundamental nature of language and what it means to know a language is still remarkably current.

Form and Meaning in Natural Languages is written in a highly academic style with long, complex sentences. You might also encounter a lot of unfamiliar vocabulary. Reading it might be hard work. For this reason, the excerpt is quite short compared to other readings. If you get lost in the long sentences, you might try to break them down into a series of shorter sentences and eliminate grammatical connectors and phrases that are just meant as side comments. For instance, the first sentence can be broken down like this:

1. When we study human language, we are approaching ~~what some might call~~ the "human essence."

2. Human essence means the distinctive qualities of mind that are ~~so for as we know~~, unique to man.

3. These qualities are inseparable from any critical phase of human existence, personal or social.

Read the excerpt at least two times. Then, pick out the main idea, and underline it.

1   When we study human language, we are approaching what some might call the "human essence," the distinctive qualities of mind that are, so far as we know, unique to man and that are inseparable[15] from any critical phase of human existence, personal or social. Hence the fascination[16] of this study, and, no less, its frustration[17]. The frustration arises from the fact that despite much progress, we remain as incapable as ever before of coming to grips with[18] the core problem of human language, which I take to be this: Having mastered a language, one is able to understand an indefinite number of expressions that are new to one's experience, that bear no simple physical resemblance[19] and are in no simple way analogous to the expressions that constitute one's linguistic[20] experience; and one is able, with greater or less facility, to produce such expressions on an appropriate occasion, despite their novelty[21] and independently of detectable stimulus[22] configurations[23], and to be understood by others who share this still mysterious ability. The normal use of language is, in this sense, a creative activity. This creative aspect of normal language use is one fundamental factor that distinguishes human language from any known system of animal communication.

2   It is important to bear in mind that the creation of linguistic expressions that are novel[24] but appropriate is the normal mode of language use. If some individual were to restrict himself largely to a definite set of linguistic patterns, to a set of habitual responses to stimulus configurations, or to "analogies" in the sense of modern linguistics, we would regard him as mentally defective[25], as being less human than animal. He would immediately be set apart from normal humans by his inability to understand normal discourse, or to take part in it in the normal way—the normal way being innovative, free from control by external stimuli, and appropriate to new and ever changing situations.

3   It is not a novel insight that human speech is distinguished by these qualities, though it is an insight that must be recaptured time and time again. With each advance in our understanding of the mechanisms of language, thought, and behavior, comes a tendency to believe that we have found the key to understanding man's apparently unique qualities

---

[15] inseparable: impossible to separate
[16] fascination: great interest
[17] frustration: feeling of disappointment caused by continual blocking of one's goals and desires
[18] coming to grips with: dealing with in a serious way
[19] resemblance: similarity in appearance
[20] linguistic: related to language
[21] novelty: newness; originality
[22] stimulus: anything that causes a physical response
[23] configuration: a pattern or arrangement
[24] novel: new
[25] defective: imperfect; not functioning properly

of mind. These advances are real, but an honest appraisal[26] will show, I think, that they are far from providing such a key. We do not understand, and for all we know, we may never come to understand what makes it possible for a normal human intelligence to use language as an instrument for the free expression of thought and feeling; or for that matter, what qualities of mind are involved in the creative acts of intelligence that are characteristic, not unique and exceptional, in a truly human existence.

---

[26] appraisal: evaluation; assessment

Thinking Beyond the Content

Getting at the Matter

Read the text at least two times. Underline the main idea of the excerpt then answer the questions in writing. Discuss your responses with one or more partners.

1. According to Chomsky, what does it mean to say that a person has mastered a language? In other words, what kinds of things can an individual do when he or she has mastered a language? Provide support for your answer from the text and from your own personal experience.

2. Is there any passage in Chomsky's text that we might see as a critique of ALICE (from the reading, "Approximating Life")?

3. What evidence do you find in the excerpt to suggest that Chomsky might be pessimistic about the possibilities of designing a genuinely intelligent chatbot?

Critical Focus: Comparing Points of View

Reading in academic disciplines often involves encountering multiple perspectives that represent various points of agreement and disagreement. College instructors will expect students to be able to compare and contrast the opinions of different writers and to decide whether they agree or disagree with various writers; therefore, the ability to compare points of view is an important skill to master.

Two systematic approaches that you might find useful for comparing points of view on a topic are: (1) creating a chart in which you list all the similarities and all the differences between two accounts or explanations of the topic, and (2) writing an imaginary conversation between the proponents of differing points of view.

Critical Focus: Application

Comparing Readings 1 and 2, do you think that Noam Chomsky and Richard Wallace share the same view of language? Choose one of these tasks to explore this question.

1. Make a chart in which you compare and contrast the views of Wallace and Chomsky on the nature of human language use.

2. Write a hypothetical dialogue between Chomsky and Wallace that illustrates in as much detail as possible the differences between the two scientists with respect to their assumptions about language.

Academic Vocabulary Focus

Following are 12 words from the AWL that appear in the reading "Form and Meaning in Natural Languages." Each word is followed by a series of words or phrases. All but one of these words or phrases express roughly the same idea as the first word. Circle the one word or phrase that is most unlike the others. Paragraph numbers are given in case you want to find the word and see how it is used in the reading. Consult a dictionary only if necessary.

analogous (Par. 1):	alike	comparable	similar	different
aspect (Par. 1):	characteristic	examination	feature	part
constitute (Par. 1):	comprise	form	control	make up
core (Par. 1):	center	difficult	heart	main
detectable (Par. 1):	invisible	measurable	noticeable	obvious
facility (Par. 1):	ability	competence	skill	speed
incapable (Par. 1):	helpless	impractical	powerless	unable
innovative (Par. 2):	creative	inventive	curious	original
insight (Par. 3):	discovery	impression	perceptive view	understanding
involve (Par. 3):	be interested in	be part of	be mixed up with	include
restrict (Par. 2):	act freely	confine	hold back	limit
unique (Par. 1, 3):	distinctive	exclusive	only one of a kind	universal

For Discussion

Discuss the questions with a partner or small group.

1. Whose view of language do you find more persuasive, that of Richard Wallace or that of Noam Chomsky?

2. The history of science is full of examples of ideas that at one time were considered foolish and impossible, for example, the idea of humans flying. Do you believe that it will someday be possible to design an artificial life form that could duplicate the language ability of the average human? Why or why not?

Reading 3

Pre-Reading

Before reading the selection, discuss the questions with a partner or small group.

1. Are there human body parts that can be replaced through modern surgical procedures? If so, which ones?

2. Do you think the replacement of a body part by a mechanical device changes the person in any fundamental way? Is there any body part that could not be replaced without fundamentally changing the person?

READING 3: Designing the Superman

Isaac Asimov

From Asimov, I. (1975). Science past—Science future. *Garden City, NY: Doubleday, pp. 226–229.*

A biochemist by training, Isaac Asimov was one of the most productive and successful writers of popular science books and science fiction in the 20th century. Asimov wrote in a simple style and with delightful humor, making scientific topics easily accessible to the general reader. In his science fiction, he often raised thought-provoking questions about the ethical implications of science. *Designing the Superman* is just such an article. The importance of this essay is not that it discusses the medical possibilities of cybernetics. Medical science has already achieved some of the breakthroughs that Asimov anticipated in his 1974 essay. The essay is really about the nature of the human being and the ethical implications of bionics[27]. In *Designing the Superman*, Asimov carries bionic engineering to its logical conclusion. In this respect, the piece is as timely today as it was when Asimov first wrote it, even if some of the references to popular culture are somewhat dated.

---

[27] bionics: the engineering of artificial systems that have biological characteristics

1 Steve Austin, the hero of the TV show "The Six Million Dollar Man,"[28] is Superman[29] born again.

2 Austin, however, hits closer to home. Superman's great talents are there only because he was born on Krypton. Since Krypton is purely mythical, none of us can be born there, and Superman can only remain a dream.

3 Austin, however, is a superman because a barely living bodily remnant[30] was stitched[31] together, and to it were added mechanical parts of great durability[32] and power and with the capacity for delicate control. It cost (in the fictional[33] world of the show) six million dollars.

4 What about real life, then? Can millionaires have themselves made into supermen? If not now, ten years from now, perhaps? And will the price be lowered to the point where someday the average junior executive, construction worker, and housewife can afford it?

5 It's not at all a strange thought, since it is only the culmination[34] of what mankind has been doing for a few hundred years. Improving this fragile[35] and ultradestructible[36] body of ours is, in fact, the name of the game we call mankind.

6 Every tool we have represents an improved body part. The stone ax is an improved fist, and the stone knife is an improved fingernail. The armor of the medieval knight was an improved skin, and gunpowder is an improved biceps for throwing missiles.

7 These are all external to the body, though. Then tools are faithless mercenaries who will work for anyone who seizes them and who will destroy today the person they were helping yesterday.

8 There are personal aids, designed to improve the parts of one particular person. There are spectacles to help the eyes, hearing aids to help the ear, chemicals to help the immunity mechanisms.

---

[28] *Six-Million-Dollar Man:* an American television series from 1974 to 1978 about a former astronaut, involved in a serious accident, who has various body parts replaced with bionic parts that give him enhanced abilities.

[29] Superman: a comic book superhero created in 1932. Superman had tremendous strength and the ability to fly. He was originally from the fictional planet Krypton but was sent to earth where he protected the people of the fictional city of Metropolis.

[30] remnant: a very small part of something that remains after the whole from which it came is gone

[31] stitch: connect by sewing

[32] durability: the ability of something to last for a long time without decreasing in strength and quality

[33] fictional: something created by imagination

[34] culmination: bringing or reaching the end of something

[35] fragile: easily damaged

[36] ultradestructable: very easily destroyed

Thinking Beyond the Content

9 Such things only help established organs. They supplement but do not replace. And if the organ fails altogether, that's it. Spectacles won't help a blind man.

10 Still closer and more intimate[37] is the pacemaker, which can be implanted in the heart and which can keep the ailing organic pump beating properly by the pacemaker's rhythmic electrical discharges[38].

11 But then why not an artificial heart altogether, and artificial kidneys, and artificial lungs? Why shouldn't devices of metal and plastic and polymer be made that are more durable and more reliable than the soft and precarious tissue parts that now exist within our skins?

12 Actually, you can build devices that will do what our various individual organs will do, but the problem is to control them. Once in the body, how do you make the artificial parts work to suit one's personal convenience? How can you become aware of the light patterns an artificial eye is recording? How can you make an artificial muscle contract by a mere effort of will? How can you make a heartbeat adjust automatically to your level of activity?

13 There we have to call in the modern electronic capacities of science. We have to insert tiny electronic devices that can be hooked to the nerves and that can be controlled by altering the nerve impulses in such a way as to duplicate[39] the natural controls of the natural body. It is something we can't quite do yet, but toward which scientists are working with considerable success.

14 A body can, in other words, control its mechanical parts by means of feedback[40]. Their activity will adjust to the information brought in by the various sensory parts.

15 The study of methods for control by feedback is called "cybernetics." If a man's organs are replaced by mechanical devices that are cybernetically controlled, what we have is a "cybernetic organism" or, taking the first syllable of each word, a "cyborg."

16 In order to make a cyborg possible, we must depend on the brain. This is natural, since the brain is the essence[41] of an individual. We have no difficulty in deciding that John Smith with a wooden leg or a glass eye is still John Smith. Part after part of the body could be replaced by a durable[42], versatile[43] mechanism, and the person is *still* John Smith, as long as the brain is left untouched and as long as all those mechanical parts are responsive to the commands of that brain. John Smith will still feel himself to be "I," as much "I" as he ever was.

---

[37] intimate: very personal or private
[38] rhythmic electrical discharges: giving off electricity pulses at regular intervals
[39] duplicate: to make an exact copy
[40] feedback: the process of sending information to a control system that will make adjustments to the operations or actions of the system
[41] essence: unique quality that makes some thing what it is
[42] durable: long lasting
[43] versatile: having many uses

17   The ultimate cyborg, then, will consist of a man's brain, spinal chord, and as much of his nerves as are necessary, placed within an utterly mechanical body that it controls.

18   Such a cyborg can be visualized as a superman indeed, if the parts are properly designed. He can be incredibly strong by ordinary human standards, incredibly quick, incredibly versatile. As long as the brain is protected, he would be able to endure hard environments. He could explore other worlds with little in the way of life-supporting equipment. With nuclear energy for power, such a cyborg would have to supply oxygen only for the brain, and could remain in outer space far more easily than he could now.

19   In fact, come to think of it, the brain is a serious drawback[44]. It *does* require protection from heat, cold, vacuum, and so on. It *must* be supplied with oxygen and glucose[45] (and quite a bit of it, too, for the brain consumes a third as much oxygen as the rest of the body put together).

20   Worse yet, the brain dies. You are born with 100 billion or so brain cells, and that is your total lifetime supply. Some of them will die; in fact, some of them are constantly dying, but no new ones will be formed. Even if all other forms of death are precluded[46], a century of life will find you far gone on the road to senility[47].

21   Can we conquer senility some day? Perhaps, but there is as yet no hint that we will be able to do so; and there is a lot more than a hint that we can do something else— replace the brain altogether.

22   We are building computers that are more and more elaborate[48] and versatile and that are more and more compact[49]. Clearly, we will someday be able to build a computer that is as complex (or even more complex) than the human brain and that is as compact (or even more compact). There are no theoretical reasons why we can't, although there are, of course, considerable engineering difficulties in the way.

23   The time will come, then, when a cyborg's brain will become useless and, instead of discarding[50] a perfectly useful body, there will be inserted a mechanical brain that is just as good as, or better than, the organic one had been in its prime. Now the cyborg is all cyb and no org.

24   And if this can be done, why not make cybs to begin with?

25   That, perhaps, is the natural route of evolution. First, there is the hit-and-miss blind-ness of natural evolution, which takes billions of years to produce some species that is

---

[44] drawback: disadvantage
[45] glucose: a simple sugar produced by plants
[46] precluded: prevented from happening
[47] senility: state of physical and mental decline usually associated with old age
[48] elaborate: complex, complicated
[49] compact: having parts that are small and arranged very closely together
[50] discard: throw away

Thinking Beyond the Content

intelligent enough to begin a directed evolution, making use of advanced biochemical and cybernetic knowledge. The intelligent species then deliberately evolves itself into a cyborg and then into a cyb (or "robot," to use another term).

26   Perhaps all over the universe there are many millions of intelligent species that have evolved into cybs and that are waiting, with considerable excitement, to see if Homo sapiens[51], here on Earth, can manage it, too.

27   And then, when we have gone from org to cyborg to cyb, from man to robot, we may finally be allowed to join the great universal brotherhood of mind that (for all we know) represents the peak and acme[52] of what life has striven for since creation.

---

[51] Homo sapiens: the Latin/scientific name for humans
[52] peak and acme: the very highest state

Critical Focus: Tracing the Steps in an Argument

Among the three general purposes of non-fiction texts are to entertain, to inform, and to persuade. Persuasive texts are designed to get readers to rethink their beliefs or opinions on a topic and come to an agreement with the writer. Persuasive texts often lead the reader through a series of steps from propositions that are easier to accept to propositions that are more difficult to accept. You can improve your comprehension and critical judgment of a persuasive text by slowing down and closely observing the movement of the text through the sequence of propositions that make up the argument. One technique that you may find useful combines two processes: 1) summarizing a passage and 2) reflecting on the purpose of the passage.

Here is how it works. First read the text one or more times to get a general idea of the argument. Then reread the text systematically, stopping after every paragraph or every several paragraphs to reflect on the movement of the argument. Try to find the divisions between steps in the argument. Ask and answer two questions at each step along the way:

- What does the passage say? (Summarize the passage in your own words.)
- What does the passage do? (State the purpose of the passage. Try to explain how the passage moves the argument forward or how it contributes to the whole argument.)

For an example of how to do this, see the Critical Focus Application exercise that follows.

Critical Focus: Application

Reread the article by Asimov, dividing it into sections according to the steps Asimov takes in his argument. At each step, write your answer to the two questions: What does it say? What does it do? Several lines within the exercise have been filled in for you to help you get started.

Paragraphs 1–3

What does it say? *Superman is completely unreal, but Steve Austin seems more possible.*

What does it do? *Compares two men with superhuman abilities. Gets the reader thinking about a fictional situation. Suggests that the main obstacle to the Austin scenario is cost.*

Paragraph 4

What does it say? _____

_____

What does it do? *Moves the fictional situation closer to the real world.*

Paragraphs 5

What does it say? _____

_____

What does it do? _____

_____

Paragraph 6

What does it say? _____

_____

What does it do? _____

_____

Continue this exercise in a notebook or on a piece of paper of your own. After you finish, discuss your work with a partner or a small group.

Getting at the Matter

Answer these questions in writing. Then discuss your responses with one or more partners.

1. Asimov sees the possibility of an evolutionary path for mankind driven by technology. What are the three stages in this evolution? (Hint: He summarizes this evolutionary path in the last paragraph.) Explain in your own words what happens at each stage.
2. Some of Asimov's claims seem easier to agree with than other claims. Which claims seem relatively easy to agree with? Which claims might be harder for a reader to agree with? How does he organize these claims and why do you think he organizes them in this way?
3. One purpose of Asimov's essay seems to be to provoke the reader into thinking critically about what it means to be human. In particular, the article raises questions about the nature of personal identity and the boundaries between man and machine. How does Asimov accomplish these purposes?
4. How would you describe the tone of this essay? Do you think Asimov is entirely serious? Is there any evidence that Asimov might be "playing" with the reader?

Academic Vocabulary Focus

In the chart that follows are 15 words from the AWL that appear in "Designing the Superman" along with the paragraph numbers where they are found. Find each word in the reading, and examine how it is used. Consult a dictionary, if necessary, to check your work. Then supply an example in which you use the word in way similar to the way it is used in the reading. The first one has been done for you as an example.

Word	Part of Speech	Meaning/Examples of Use
adjust (to) (Par. 12, 14)	*verb*	*to make changes so two things are in balance/ It may be a little time before you can **adjust** properly to the different pace of life. (Adapted from a Collins Cobuild example.)*
altering (Par. 13)		
aware (of) (Par. 12)		
capacities (Par. 3, 13)		

considerable (Par. 13, 22, 26)		
designed (Par. 8, 18)		
established (Par. 9)		
insert (Par. 13, 23)		
mechanism (Par. 8, 16)		
prime (Par. 23)		
consume (Par. 19)		
reliable (Par. 11)		
supplement (Par. 9)		
ultimate (Par. 17)		
visualize (Par. 18)		

For Discussion

Discuss these questions with a partner or small group.

1. Asimov does not discuss possible objections to his argument. Make a list of the objections that might be raised to the serious pursuit of a project involving the development of cybernetic "life-forms?" (Hint: Try to imagine what kinds of problems might arise: social, political, legal, and ethical as a result of having a population of cybernetic life-forms living among ordinary people.)

2. Do you think Richard Wallace would feel more comfortable in the company of Isaac Asimov or Noam Chomsky? Explain.

For Further Investigation

1. Use library or Internet sources to find out more about Alan Turing or Marvin Minsky.

2. Use library or Internet sources to find out more about Zipf's Law. What other phenomena besides word frequencies seem to obey Zipf's law?

3. Who was Isaac Asimov? Find out more about his life and his work.

4. Who is Noam Chomsky? What can you find out about his contributions to modern linguistic theory?

5. What science fiction books, movies, or TV serials deal with topics or issues similar to the issues taken up in "Designing the Superman"? Make a list and give brief summaries for each title on your list.

6. *Androids, cyborgs,* and *robots* are terms for describing similar entities. Are there any differences between these entities? What is currently real and what is fictional in this area?

3: Global Health Issues

Globalization refers to the increasing interconnectedness of societies around the world. This greater interconnectedness is a result of technological changes that have increased the speed and efficiency of global transportation and communication. At the same time, countries have continued to reform trade policies making it easier to export products around the world. In this unit, you will explore some effects of these historical trends as they relate to global health.

The first reading, "Global Trends in Tobacco Use," is an excerpt from a report produced by an international team of economists, public health specialists, social scientists, public policy analysts, and legal experts. The report was published by the World Bank, an organization that provides financial and technical assistance to developing countries around the world. The reading highlights concerns regarding the growing number of tobacco smokers, particularly in the developing countries of the world.

In the second reading, "The Human-Animal Link," two prominent veterinarians with the Wildlife Conservation Society, argue that preventing global epidemics of infectious disease requires a recognition of the interdependence of humans, domestic animals, and wildlife.

In the final reading, "On Being an Adolescent in the 21st Century," Paul F. A. Van Look, Director of Reproductive Health and Research at the World Health Organization, outlines the major health risks facing adolescents around the world, focusing especially on sexual and reproductive health issues.

Reading 1

Pre-Reading

Before reading the selection, discuss the questions with a partner or small group.

1. What health risks are associated with tobacco use?

2. Do you think that tobacco use is more common in affluent[1] countries or poor countries?

3. Do you think tobacco-related illnesses are likely to become more or less common in the future? Why?

---

[1] affluent: having plenty of money, wealthy

READING 1: Global Trends in Tobacco Use

Prabhat Jha and Frank J. Chaloupka

Excerpt from Jha, P., & Chaloupka, F. J. (1999). Curbing the epidemic: Governments and the economics of tobacco control. *Washington, DC: The World Bank, pp. 13–19.*

The mission of the World Bank is to provide financial and technical assistance to developing countries around the world in order to reduce global poverty and promote economic development. The World Bank recognizes that tobacco-related diseases place an economic burden on countries where tobacco use is high. This economic burden is particularly problematic for developing countries. For this reason, the World Bank has had an official policy, since 1991, of not providing financial support for tobacco production. The reading that follows is an excerpt from a report intended to offer policymakers in developing countries insight into the economic benefits of tobacco control.

Most of the data in this article were gathered during the 1990s and represent trends that were apparent throughout the '90s. Therefore, it may not accurately reflect the most current developments. However, it is important to understand that large-scale data-gathering projects are difficult and often operate over periods of a decade or more. The United States Census Bureau, for instance, collects data describing many characteristics of the U.S. population once every 10 years; the next census will not occur until 2010. Between these major "decennial" surveys, the Census Bureau conducts smaller-scale surveys on specific issues like health, crime, or employment. The gathering of accurate data on worldwide trends in tobacco use is a similarly large project, and the World Bank report probably represents the best data available through the mid- to late 2000s when *Thinking Beyond the Content* was in preparation. Moreover, demographic trends do not often change dramatically over the short term.

1   Although people have used tobacco for centuries, cigarettes did not appear in mass-manufactured form until the 19th century. Since then, the practice of cigarette smoking has spread worldwide on a massive scale. Today about one in three adults, or 1.1 billion people, smoke. Of these, about 80 percent live in low- and middle-income countries. Partly because of growth in the adult population, and partly because of increased consumption, the total number of smokers is expected to reach about 1.6 billion by 2025.

2   In the past, tobacco was often chewed or smoked in various kinds of pipes. While these practices persist, they are declining. Manufactured cigarettes and various types of hand-rolled cigarette such as bidis—common in Southeast Asia and India—now account for up to 85 percent of all tobacco consumed worldwide. Cigarette smoking appears to pose much greater dangers to health than earlier forms of tobacco use. This report therefore focuses on manufactured cigarettes and bidis.

Rising Consumption in Low-Income and Middle-Income Countries

3   The populations of the low- and middle-income countries have been increasing their cigarette consumption since about 1970 (see Figure 1.1). The per capita[2] consumption in these countries climbed steadily between 1970 and 1990, although the upward trend may have slowed a little since the early 1990s.

FIGURE 1.1   Smoking is Increasing in Developing World.

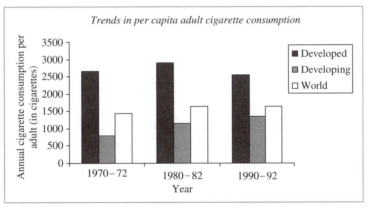

Source: World Health Organization, 1997. *Tobacco or Health: A Global Status Report.* Geneva, Switzerland. Ommy nummole ssequis sequat.

4   While the practice of smoking has become more prevalent[3] among men in low- and middle-income countries, it has been in overall decline among men in the high-income countries during the same period. For example, more than 55 percent of men in the United States smoked at the peak[4] of consumption in the mid-20th century, but the proportion had fallen to 28 percent by the mid-1990s. Per capita consumption for the populations of the high-income countries as a whole also has dropped. However, among certain groups in these countries, such as teenagers and young women, the proportion who smokes has grown in the 1990s. Overall,

---

[2] per capita: for each person
[3] prevalent: common, frequently occurring
[4] peak: highest point or level

then, the smoking epidemic is spreading from its original focus, among men in high-income countries, to women in high-income countries and men in low-income regions.

5   In recent years, international trade agreements have liberalized[5] global trade in many goods and services. Cigarettes are no exception. The removal of trade barriers[6] tends to introduce greater competition that results in lower prices, greater advertising and promotion, and other activities that stimulate demand[7]. One study concluded that in four Asian economies that opened their markets in response to U.S. trade pressure during the 1980s—Japan, South Korea, Taiwan, and Thailand—consumption of cigarettes per person was almost 10 percent higher in 1991 than it would have been if these markets had remained closed. An econometric model[8] developed for this report concludes that increased trade liberalization contributed significantly to increases in cigarette consumption, particularly in the low- and middle-income countries.

Regional Patterns in Smoking

6   Data on the number of smokers in each region have been compiled by the World Health Organization using more than 80 separate studies. For the purpose of this report, these data have been used to estimate the prevalence of smoking in each of the seven World Bank country groupings. As Table 1.1 shows, there are wide variations between regions and, in particular, in the prevalence of smoking among women in different regions. For example, in Eastern Europe and Central Asia (mainly the former socialist economies), 59 percent of men and 26 percent of women smoked in 1995, more than in any other region. Yet in East Asia and the Pacific, where the prevalence of male smoking is equally high, at 59 percent, just 4 percent of women were smokers.

Smoking and Socioeconomic Status

7   Historically, as incomes rose within populations, the number of people who smoked rose too. In the earlier decades of the smoking epidemic in high-income countries, smokers were more likely to be affluent than poor. But in the past three to four decades, this pattern appears to have been reversed, at least among men, for whom data are widely available. Affluent men in the high-income countries have increasingly abandoned tobacco, whereas poorer men have not done so. For example, in Norway, the percentage of men with high incomes who smoked fell from 75 percent in 1955 to 28 percent in 1990. Over the same period, the proportion of men on low incomes who smoked declined much less steeply[9], from 60 percent in 1955 to 48 percent in 1990. Today, in most high-income

---

[5] liberalized: reformed something to make it less strict
[6] trade barriers: rules that prevent or restrict trade
[7] stimulate demand: encourage desire for a product
[8] econometric model: a tool using economic statistics to explain
[9] decline steeply: decreased by a large amount

Thinking Beyond the Content

Table 1.1 Regional Patterns of Smoking

Estimated smoking prevalence by gender and number of smokers in population age 15 or more, by World Bank region, 1995.					
World Bank Region Smoking Prevalence (Percentage)					
	Males	**Females**	**Overall**	**Total Smokers (millions)**	**(Percentage of All Smokers)**
East Asia and Pacific	59	4	32	401	35
Eastern Europe and Central Asia	59	26	41	148	13
Latin America and Caribbean	40	21	30	95	8
Middle East and North Africa	44	5	25	40	3
South Asia (cigarettes)	20	1	11	86	8
South Asia (bidis)	20	3	12	96	8
Sub-Saharan Africa	33	10	21	67	6
Low/Middle Income	49	9	29	933	82
High Income	39	22	30	209	18
World	47	12	29	1,142	100

*Note: Numbers have been rounded.
Source: Author's calculations based on World Health Organization, 1997. *Tobacco or Health: A Global Status Report.* Geneva, Switzerland.

countries, there are significant differences in the prevalence of smoking between different socioeconomic groups. In the United Kingdom, for instance, only 10 percent of women and 12 percent of men in the highest socioeconomic group are smokers; in the lowest socioeconomic groups the corresponding figures are threefold greater: 35 percent and 40 percent. The same inverse relationship is found between education levels—a marker for socioeconomic status—and smoking. In general, individuals who have received little or no education are more likely to smoke than those who are more educated.

8   Until recently, it was thought that the situation in low- and middle-income countries was different. However, the most recent research concludes that here too, men of low socioeconomic status are more likely to smoke than those of high socioeconomic status. Educational level is a clear determinant of smoking in Chennai, India (Figure 1.2). Studies in Brazil, China, South Africa, Vietnam, and several Central American nations confirm this pattern.

FIGURE 1.2   Smoking Is More Common among the Less Educated.

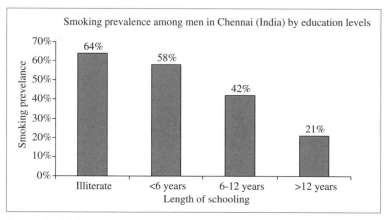

Smoking prevalence among men in Chennai (India) by education levels

Source: Gajalakshmi, C. K., P. Jha, S. Nguyen, and A. Yurekli. *Patterns of Tobacco Use, and Health Consequences.* Background paper.

9   While it is thus clear that the prevalence of smoking is higher among the poor and less educated worldwide, there are fewer data on the number of cigarettes smoked daily by different socioeconomic groups. In high-income countries, with some exceptions, poor and less educated men smoke more cigarettes per day than richer, more educated men. While it might have been expected that poor men in low- and middle-income countries would smoke fewer cigarettes than affluent men, the available data indicate that, in general, smokers with low levels of education consume equal or slightly larger numbers of cigarettes than those with high levels of education. An important exception is India, where, not surprisingly, smokers with college-level education status tend to consume more cigarettes, which are relatively more expensive, while smokers with low levels of education status consume larger numbers of the inexpensive bidis.

Age and the Uptake[10] of Smoking

10   It is unlikely that individuals who avoid starting to smoke in adolescence or young adulthood will ever become smokers. Nowadays, the overwhelming majority of smokers start before age 25, often in childhood or adolescence (see Box 1.1 and Figure 1.3); in the high-income countries, eight out of 10 begin in their teens. In middle-income and low-income countries for which data are available, it appears that most smokers start by the early twenties, but the trend is toward younger ages. For example, in China between 1984 and 1996, there was a significant increase in the number of young men aged between 15 and 19 years who took up smoking. A similar decline in the age of starting has been observed in the high-income countries.

---

[10] uptake: to start or begin doing something

Thinking Beyond the Content

FIGURE 1.3   Smoking Starts Early in Life.

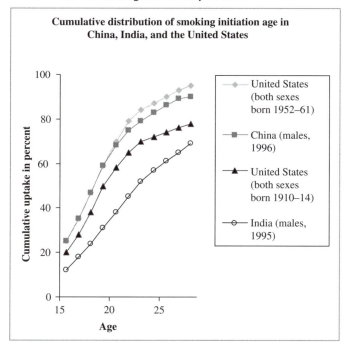

Cumulative distribution of smoking initiation age in China, India, and the United States

Legend:
- United States (both sexes born 1952–61)
- China (males, 1996)
- United States (both sexes born 1910–14)
- India (males, 1995)

Y-axis: Cumulative uptake in percent
X-axis: Age

Sources: Chinese Academy of Preventive Medicine, 1997. *Smoking in China: 1996 National Prevalence Survey of Smoking Pattern.* Beijing. Science and Technology Press; Gupta, P.C., 1996. "Survey of Sociodemographic Characteristics of Tobacco Use among 99,598 Individuals in Bombay, India, Using Handheld Computers." Tobacco Control 5:114–20, and U.S. Surgeon General Reports, 1989 and 1994.

Global Patterns of Quitting

11   While there is evidence that smoking begins in youth worldwide, the proportion of smokers who quit appears to vary sharply between high-income countries and the rest of the world, at least to date. In environments of steadily increased knowledge about the health effects of tobacco, the prevalence of smoking has gradually fallen and a significant number of former smokers have accumulated over the decades. In most high-income countries, about 30 percent of the male population are former smokers. In contrast, only 2 percent of Chinese men had quit in 1993, only 5 percent of Indian males at around the same period, and only 10 percent of Vietnamese males had quit in 1997.

Box 1.1 How Many Young People Take Up Smoking Each Day?

Individuals who start to smoke at a young age are likely to become heavy smokers and are also at increased risk of dying from smoking-related diseases in later life. It is therefore important to know how many children and young people take up smoking daily. We attempt here to answer this question.

We used (1) World Bank data on the number of children and adolescents, male and female, who reached age 20 in 1995, for each World Bank region, and (2) data from the World Health Organization on the prevalence of smokers in all age groups up to the age of 30 in each of these regions. For an upper estimate, we assumed that the number of young people who take up smoking every day is a product of 1x2 per region, for each gender. For a lower estimate, we reduced this by region-specific estimates for the number of smokers who start after the age of 30.

We made three conservative assumptions: First, that there have been minimal changes over time in the average age of uptake. There have been recent downward trends in the age of uptake in young Chinese men, but assuming little change means that, if anything, our figures are underestimates. Second, we focused on regular smokers, excluding the much larger number of children who would try smoking but not become regular smokers. Third, we assumed that, for those young people who become regular smokers, quitting before adulthood is rare. While the number of adolescent regular smokers who quit is substantial in high-income countries, in low- and middle-income countries it is currently very low.

With these assumptions, we calculated that the number of children and young people taking up smoking ranges from 14,000 to 15,000 per day in the high-income countries as a whole. For middle- and low-income countries, the estimated numbers range from 68,000 to 84,000. This means that every day, worldwide, there are between 82,000 and 99,000 young people starting to smoke and risking rapid addiction to nicotine[11] These figures are consistent with existing estimates for individual high-income countries.

---

[11] nicotine: a toxic chemical found in tobacco

Thinking Beyond the Content

Critical Focus: Reading the Graphs and Tables in a Text

Academic texts, especially in the sciences and social *s*ciences, often incorporate graphs and tables in which data relevant to the topic are displayed. As a reader, it is important to pay attention to both the text and any accompanying graphs. Writers often discuss the data contained in these graphs and tables, and these discussions can help a reader understand the graphs. At the same time, studying the graphs can help the reader understand the main ideas and important details of the text that are based on data.

For example, Paragraphs 3 and 4 of the reading discuss per capita cigarette consumption in high-income versus low- and middle-income countries. These paragraphs indicate that per capita cigarette consumption is going up in the low- and middle-income countries and down in the high-income countries, but the text doesn't indicate where per capita consumption is greater. The graph in Figure 1.1, however, quickly makes the relationship clear. The graph clearly shows that smokers in the developed world (i.e., the wealthier countries) actually consume more cigarettes per person. The main point of the paragraph, that per capita consumption is growing in the developing (low-middle income) countries while it is falling in the developed (i.e., high income) countries is further emphasized by the graph.

In reading a graph, it is important to gain a clear understanding of the elements of the graph or table.

- Read the title and legend carefully. The title will provide a general description of the graph represents, and the legend will identify each data set plotted in the graph.
- It is also important to pay special attention to units of measurement for the results. For instance, does the numeral 1,000 represent merely 1,000 or 1,000 millions, or some other quantity? You will need to read the category title for each data set on the horizontal x-axis and the vertical y-axis.
- Line graphs are used to show how something changes over time. For example, a scientist may be gathering data once a year on the population of a species of bird found in a specific area over a period of five years. After the data are gathered, a line graph can be used to show how this population changes over time. In some cases, the scientist may have

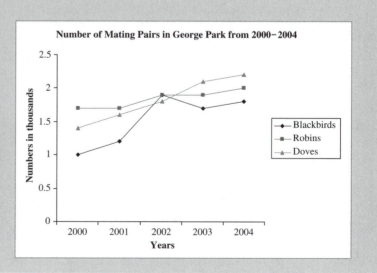

several lines on the same graph showing how other related variables changed over the same period. For example, the graph on page 87 shows the number of mating pairs of birds for three species. While it is clear that all bird populations have increased, some bird populations have done better than others during each year, category title for y-axis of the five-year period shown on x-axis. Notice that the population counts on the y-axis are in thousands.

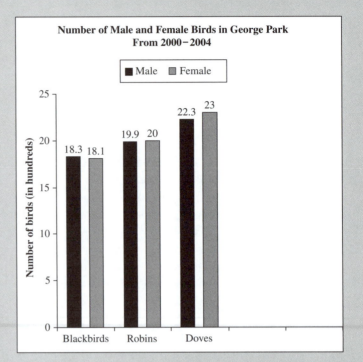

Number of Male and Female Birds in George Park From 2000−2004

- A bar graph is used to show differences among categories of data. In general, one category does not necessarily affect another in any way. This is a useful type of graph for determining how various categories differ. For example, looking at the total population of each type of bird may not be enough. The scientist may want to show how many birds in the park were male and how many were female for each of the species. A bar graph can be used to show this information. In the graph above, it is clear that the overall female population of birds is greater than the males. However, it is also clear that the number of female birds is only greater in the robin and dove populations. Noticethat the x-axis shows species and differentiates between males and females by using differently shaded bars. Also notice that the numbers repre-sented in the y-axis are in hun-dreds instead of the thousands shown on the graph on page 87.

- Pie charts or circle graphs are used to compare parts of the whole with each other, or the fraction of the whole each part takes up. The numbers shown are often in percentages and equal 100 when totaled. In other words, as one number increases, another must decrease until 100 percent is reached. Using a pie graph, a

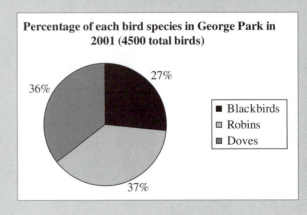

Percentage of each bird species in George Park in 2001 (4500 total birds)

27%
36%
37%

- Blackbirds
- Robins
- Doves

Thinking Beyond the Content

scientist can show just what portion of all the birds in the park are from which particular species or the total male population in relation to the female population. The pie graph on page 88 clearly shows that robins represent the greatest population of birds in the park, with doves coming in a close second.

Explaining the information in a graph to another person is a good way to check your understanding of the graph. Here is a systematic way to discuss the information in a graph:

1. Give the title or a one-sentence explanation of the purpose of the graph.

2. Explain what the x-axis and the y-axis represent.

3. Explain any symbols used to differentiate categories of data.

4. Explain one or two specific data points that illustrate the type of data shown.

5. Explain what general trend or message is evident from the graph overall.

Critical Focus: Application

Work with a partner.

1. Each member of the group will choose one of the graphs or tables that accompany this reading or one from the Critical Focus box above and explain the information contained in it to the other members of the group.

2. Do an Internet search on "Global Trends in Tobacco Use," and locate three or four graphs related to this subject. Bring copies to class and explain the information contained in them to the other members of the class.

Getting at the Matter

Write a brief (one paragraph) answer to each of the questions.

1. Describe the regional trends in global tobacco use.

2. Describe the changes in the demographic characteristics (e.g., gender and socioeconomic characteristics) of tobacco users worldwide.

3. What do we know about uptake of smoking? What implications do you see for public health professionals who would like to discourage tobacco uptake?

4. What are the likely consequences of free trade on cigarette consumption?

5. What kinds of trends have been observed in global patterns of quitting?

6. For which countries does cigarette smoking pose the greatest public health concern? What predictions can you make about future tobacco-related disease patterns in these countries based on the trends reported in this reading?

Academic Vocabulary Focus

A selection of words from the Academic Word List (AWL) that appear in the reading "Global Trends in Tobacco Use" follows. Check off the words that you already know. If there are any words that you do not know, use the paragraph numbers to locate these words in the reading and use a dictionary to determine their meaning. Complete the chart by adding related word forms for each word.

Noun	Verb	Adjective	Adverb
		available (Par. 7, 9, 10)	
	compile (Par. 6)		
		consistent (Box 1.1)	
	contribute (Par. 5)		____
		corresponding (Par. 7)	
data (Par. 6, 7, 9, 10)	____	data	____
liberalization (Par. 5)		liberalized (Par. 5)	
proportion (Par. 4, 7, 11)	____		
region (Par. 4, 6)			
source (Table 1.1)	source	source	____
____		specific (Box 1.1)	
variation (Par. 6)	vary (Par. 11)		

Complete the sentences related to the reading by choosing the correct form of the word in parentheses.

1. The wide (available) _____ of data on smoking prevalence rates among men gives public health workers a good idea of smoking trends among men. Data on smoking rates among women are just beginning to be more widely _____.

2. The World Health Organization made a (compiled) _____ of the data of more than 80 different studies of smokers in various regions.

3. The data (consistent) _____ shows that a greater percentage of people in more wealthy countries are more likely to refrain from smoking or quit smoking compared to people in poorer countries.

4. Research by the World Health Organization has (contribute) _____ to a better understanding of which groups of people are at higher risk for smoking.

5. It is becoming increasingly clear that the likelihood of someone starting to smoke (corresponding) _____ to their socio-economic and educational level.

6. This may be partially due to the cheaper price of cigarettes in many countries as a result of the (liberalized) _____ of global trade.

7. While smoking is on the decline in more affluent cultures and women tend to smoke less than men in general, some (region) _____ variations are apparent from the data.

8. Table 1.1 clearly shows that for every region of the world the (proportion) _____ of women who smoke is considerably lower than the _____ of men who smoke. Unfortunately, however, smoking rates among young women are growing in some parts of the world.

9. Although socio-economic factors seem to play a part in predicting who is likely to smoke, it now appears that another factor may play a bigger role, more (specific) _____, educational level.

10. According to the text, one of the most significant (vary) _____ that has led to decreased smoking rates in the developed world is increased knowledge about the health risks of tobacco use.

For Discussion

Discuss the questions in a small group. Choose one member of your group to summarize for the whole class the opinions expressed in your group's discussion.

1. To what extent is tobacco smoking regulated in your country? Is smoking prohibited in any public places? If so, where is it permitted, and where is it prohibited?

2. Is tobacco advertising permitted on television in your country? Do you think the advertising of tobacco on TV should or should not be permitted?

3. Is there a minimum age for buying tobacco in your country? If so, what is it?

4. Given the well-documented health risks associated with tobacco, why do many young people still take up smoking?

Reading 2

Pre-Reading

Before reading the selection, discuss the questions with a partner or small group.

1. Name as many infectious diseases as you can that are dangerous for global health.

2. Which, if any, of these diseases originate in animals and spread to humans? List as many possible consequences of such diseases as you can.

Thinking Beyond the Content

For this next reading, our Critical Focus consists of two techniques with which every critical reader should be familiar: Previewing and Annotating a Text. These techniques can be useful for helping the reader handle a wide range of texts, but they are particularly useful for long, complex readings. Since we recommend that you try them on the next reading, we are changing the usual order of unit elements. Instead of introducing the Critical Focus after the reading as we have done previously throughout the book, we will introduce it before the reading so that you may try these techniques on the reading, which is rather long and complex.

Critical Focus: Previewing a Text

Previewing is a technique that skilled readers use to help them gain a general understanding of what a text is about and how it is organized. Getting a general idea of the content and organization of a text before reading it in detail may enable you to comprehend the text more easily.

In previewing, you do not read the entire text. Instead, you look at items such as:

- information about the author
- title and subheadings
- first and last paragraph
- first and last sentences of each paragraph
- key words that may be highlighted or glossed
- diagrams, graphs and tables
- pictures and illustrations

Your goal is to understand the gist or main idea of the reading.

Critical Focus: Application

Before you read the selection that follows, preview it. Then discuss with a partner what you think the reading will be about.

After gaining a general overview of a text by previewing it, you are in a position to do a close, focused reading of it. Annotating is a technique to help you do this more intensive kind of reading.

Critical Focus: Annotating a Text

To **annotate** a text is to take notes within the text. When you annotate a text, you mark on it with pencil, pen, or colored markers. If the text is not yours to mark, you can use sticky notes. Editable electronic texts can be annotated by using commenting features available in some word processing applications or by employing drawing functions including textboxes and arrows.

You annotate a text in order to comprehend it, extract important information for some further purpose (e.g., studying or writing a research paper), or to critically analyze the content of the text. Annotating takes many forms, but some typical ways of annotating include:

- Underlining, highlighting, or circling key words, phrases, or ideas.
- Writing comments in response to ideas within the text in the margins or on sticky notes. These comments might involve expressions of agreement, disagreement, or skepticism.
- Making remarks about connections between ideas or claims in the text and other sources.
- Indicating questions you might have for later clarification.

Critical Focus: Application

As you read "The Human-Animal Link," annotate it. Follow each suggestion given in the preceding Critical Focus box. After you have read and annotated your text, compare your work with that of a partner. Discuss the information that you annotated. What did you learn from the reading? What questions or comments did you have that you might want to pursue?

READING 2: The Human-Animal Link

William B. Karesh and Robert A. Cook

Karesh, W. B., & Cook, R. A. (2005, July/August). The human and animal link. Foreign Affairs, *84(4) pp. 38–50. (A longer version of this article originally appeared in* Foreign Affairs.*)*

Among the most serious threats to global health today is the prospect of an infectious disease sweeping across every continent helped along by global trade or travel. The authors of the next article are veterinary (i.e., animal) doctors with the Wildlife Conservation Society (WCS), an organization with headquarters in New York and ongoing field projects around the world. Its mission is to provide leadership in environmental education and to conserve and protect wild animals around the world.

Cook is Vice President and Chief Veterinarian at the WCS, and Karesh is the Director of the Field Veterinary Program at WCS and Co-chair of the World Conservation Union's Veterinary Specialist Group, the world's largest conservation network headquartered in Switzerland. According to Karesh and Cook, world health authorities must think about health and disease in a more holistic way that recognizes the connection between human-health and animal-health. The issues that Karesh and Cook discuss seem likely to become ever more relevant as world population increases and intercontinental trade and travel continues to increase.

One World, One Health

1   In recent years, outbreaks of diseases such as avian flu[12], severe acute respiratory syndrome (SARS)[13], the Ebola virus[14], and mad cow disease[15] have frightened the public, disrupted global commerce, caused massive economic losses, and jeopardized[16] diplomatic relations. These diseases have also shared a worrisome key characteristic: the ability to cross the Darwinian[17] divide between animals and people. None of these illnesses depends on human hosts for its survival; as a result, they all persist today, far beyond the reach of medical intervention.

2   Diseases pay no regard to the divisions among species or academic disciplines, and the failure to recognize this truth is placing humanity in great peril[18]. As a recent outbreak of avian influenza reminded the world, what happens in one part of it—and to one species—can have a deadly serious impact on others. The planet clearly needs a new health paradigm[19] that not only integrates the efforts of disparate[20] groups but also balances their respective influences, to help bridge the gaps between them. This is especially so since the immediate effects of a particular illness are often the least of the problem. Diseases that attack people and animals also cause poverty and civil unrest, disrupt "free" ecosystem services such as drinking water and plant pollination[21], and threaten otherwise well-planned and sustainable economic development efforts, such as low-impact tourism[22]. In short, the failure to adopt a planet-wide and cross-species approach to health is getting costlier by the day; humanity cannot afford to pay the price much longer.

The World We Were Given

3   According to recent analysis, more than 60 percent of the 1,415 infectious diseases currently known to modern medicine are capable of infecting both animals and humans.

---

[12] avian flu: a viral disease found chiefly in birds, but infections can occur in humans.

[13] severe acute respiratory syndrome: a dangerous respiratory disease in humans spread by close contact

[14] Ebola virus: an incurable, deadly virus that causes high fever and massive internal bleeding

[15] mad cow disease: a deadly, infectious brain disease in cattle passed to humans through infected meat

[16] jeopardized: put in danger

[17] Darwinian: referring to Charles Darwin, the 19th century naturalist known for the theory of evolution by natural selection

[18] peril: danger

[19] paradigm: a generally accepted model of how ideas relate to one another

[20] disparate: unrelated; dissimilar

[21] pollination: the process by which plants are fertilized

[22] low-impact tourism: travel that has a minimal effect on the environment, culture, and social structures of the area visited

Thinking Beyond the Content

Most of these diseases (such as anthrax[23], Rift Valley fever[24], bubonic plague[25], Lyme disease[26], and monkeypox[27] are "zoonotic," meaning that they originated in animals but have crossed the species barrier to infect people. The others, which receive less attention, are "anthropozoonotic," meaning they are typically found in humans but can and do infect animals as well (examples include the human herpes virus, tuberculosis, and measles). Dividing infectious agents into these two groups is convenient for teaching purposes. But it overlooks the critically important fact that all of them can move back and forth among species, mutating[28] and changing their characteristics in the process. Avian influenza—which started in birds but is now infecting humans as well—has recently highlighted the need for a more holistic view of disease.

4   It is probably just luck that has so far allowed scientists to maintain these distinctions. One of the greatest medical success stories of the last century was the eradication[29] of smallpox. But this achievement was largely due to the fact that smallpox survives in only one host species, namely humans. If even one more type of animal had been able to harbor the disease, there is a good chance that eradication would not have been accomplished, despite the Herculean[30] global effort. When a pathogen[31] can find refuge or a place to mutate in a range of hosts, controlling it becomes far more complex, requiring an integrated[32]—and much more difficult—approach.

5   To get a sense of the breadth and the seriousness of the issue, consider HIV/AIDS, which most scientists now think arose in Africa as a result of the human consumption of primates that were infected with simian[33] immunodeficiency viruses. Or consider the Ebola virus, which has a similar history. The disease first came to international attention in 1976, when it appeared around the Ebola River in what was then called Zaire. The virus infects people, gorillas, chimpanzees, and monkeys, causing severe

---

[23] anthrax: an infectious bacterial disease passed from animals to humans through feces and infected meat

[24] Rift Valley fever: a fever-causing viral disease affecting domestic animals and humans, first found in the Rift Valley of Kenya in 1930

[25] bubonic plague: a fatal infectious disease transmitted by fleas

[26] Lyme disease: an infectious bacterial disease transmitted by ticks, causing skin rash, fever, and headache followed by arthritis and nervous disorder

[27] monkeypox: a rare viral disease found mostly in the rainforest countries of central and west Africa and spread to humans through infected animals

[28] mutating: undergoing a physical or biochemical change

[29] eradication: the complete elimination

[30] Herculean: relating to Hercules, a character from Greek mythology, known for his great strength, who was obliged to perform 12 nearly impossible tasks, referred to as the labors of Hercules.

[31] pathogen: something capable of causing disease, e.g., bacterium or virus

[32] integrated: made of elements working together that usually operate separately

[33] simian: referring to monkeys and apes

internal and external hemorrhaging[34] and leading to death in up to 90 percent of its human victims. Human infection spreads quickly, especially via caregivers and people who flee an area to escape the illness. Since the disease first appeared, successive human outbreaks have been recorded in Côte d'Ivoire, Gabon, Sudan, and Uganda. But humans have not been the only victims; lowland gorillas and chimpanzees in Gabon and Congo and chimpanzees in western equatorial Africa have been decimated by the sickness. Other forest animals, such as duikers (small antelopes) and bush pigs may also be affected. When subsistence hunters[35] discover a sick or dead animal in the forest, they view it as good fortune and bring it home to feed their families or trade with their neighbors. The Ebola virus then easily infects those handling the meat, and a chain of contacts and infections ensue. Each of the human outbreaks in central Africa during the late 1990s and the first years of this century was traced to humans handling infected great apes.

6   SARS also arose from contact with wild animals. The illness first appeared in late 2002 in China's Guangdong Province, where people began complaining of high fever, cough, and diarrhea, and eventually developed severe pneumonia. The unknown disease was very contagious; within a matter of weeks, a visitor to Hong Kong helped spread it to five continents. By July of 2003, the WHO [World Health Organization] had tallied 8,437 cases and 813 deaths. Due mostly to a lack of understanding of the new disease, global travel and trade were disrupted as fear spread.

7   After four months, scientists eventually discovered that the mystery disease was caused by a corona virus (a family of viruses found in many animal species). The virus, in turn, was traced back to a small mammal called the palm civet, which is farmed in the Guangdong region and sold for human consumption. Later, evidence of the virus was also found in raccoon dogs, ferrets, and badgers being sold in Guangdong's wildlife markets, as well as in domestic cats living in the city. Epidemiological[36] studies confirmed that the first human infections had indeed come through animal contact, although the exact species responsible has not been definitively identified.

8   In the months after SARS first appeared, the Chinese government closed down its live wildlife markets. Within ten days of linking the disease to the wild animal trade, the government also confiscated[37] close to a million animals, many of which had been brought into the area from other parts of the world and which hosted a variety of exotic viruses and bacteria. But the damage had already been done. Prior to the government action, the animals were often housed together, exposed to one another's waste, and sometimes

---

[34] hemorrhaging: severe bleeding

[35] subsistence hunters: people who survive primarily by hunting

[36] epidemiological: relating to the scientific study of the causes and transmission of diseases in a population

[37] confiscated: took away; seized

Thinking Beyond the Content

even fed to one another. For a virus or bacteria capable of jumping between species, the markets had provided the perfect place to reproduce.

The World's Not Flat, It's a Mixing Bowl

9 Determining the exact scale of the global wildlife trade is impossible, since the operations range from the extremely local to the international, and are often illegal and informal. Part of the picture, however, can be glimpsed[38] from figures compiled by the Wildlife Conservation Society from a variety of sources. According to these numbers, the annual global trade in live wild animals includes roughly 4 million birds, 640,000 reptiles, and 40,000 primates. Following the SARS outbreak that began in 2002, the Chinese government reportedly confiscated 838,500 wild animals from the markets of Guangdong. But every year, tens of millions of wild mammals, birds, and reptiles continue to flow through these and other trading centers, where they make contact with humans and dozens of other species before being shipped elsewhere, sold locally, or sometimes freed back into the wild—often carrying new and dangerous pathogens. The number of these animals that end up as food is staggering[39]; indeed, experts estimate that in central Africa alone consumers eat 579 million individual wild animals a year, for a total of more than a billion kilograms of meat. Meanwhile, people in the Amazon basin are thought to consume between 67 and 164 million kilograms of wild animal meat a year, accounting for between 6.4 million and 15.8 million individual mammals alone.

10 Before these animals (with whatever diseases they may be carrying) are eaten, they encounter—and possibly transmit pathogens to—hunters and marketers. They also risk infecting domestic animals and wild scavengers in villages and market areas that consume the remnants and waste of wildlife eaten by humans. All considered, at least a billion direct and indirect contacts among wildlife, humans, and domestic animals result from the handling of wildlife and the wildlife trade annually.

11 Such contact does not just endanger humans and their pets; the pathogens inadvertently[40] transported around the globe can also devastate local wildlife, disrupting the environment and causing enormous economic harm. In October 2004, avian flu (specifically, the H5N1 type A influenza virus) was detected in two mountain hawk-eagles that were smuggled from Thailand into Belgium in airline carry-on baggage. Last year, another deadly virus entered Italy via a shipment of Pakistani parrots, lovebirds, and finches. Chytridiomycosis, a fungal disease responsible for the extinction of 30 percent of the world's amphibian species, has been spread by the international trade and subsequent

---

[38] glimpsed: seen a little bit of something
[39] staggering: surprising
[40] inadvertently: by accident

release of African clawed frogs (a popular laboratory animal). Tuberculosis originating from domestic cattle has now infected herds of wild bison in Canada, deer in Michigan, and Cape buffalo and lions in South Africa. In 1999, rinderpest, a disease originally introduced to Africa by the importation of domestic cattle from India, killed more wild buffalo in Kenya than had been slain by poachers[41] during the previous two decades.

12   The increasing movement of animals and humans around the world and their greater exposure to the many diseases that dance between them have also placed domesticated livestock at increasing risk. This is especially so since the ravenous[42] international demand for animal meat has turned livestock production into an ultra intensive industry, with swine, poultry, and cattle operations now packing huge numbers of animals into limited spaces. Moreover, projections by the International Food Policy Research Institute indicate a doubling of animal production in developing countries over the next 20 years. Although modern factory-farm practices maximize food production, they also make livestock more susceptible to illness. Infection spreads quickly through crowded animal pens, and growing antibiotic resistance makes fighting disease more difficult. Many farms now routinely mix antibiotics[43] with animal feed to avoid transmitting illnesses, and selective breeding for specific traits often predisposes animals to conditions requiring repeated antibiotic treatment. Such increased antibiotic use is helping to create dangerous drug-resistant super bugs that may endanger both animals and humans.

13   High-volume food production has also prompted the livestock industry to adopt other dangerous practices, which have already led to at least one high-profile disaster: the outbreak of bovine spongiform encephalopathy (BSE), or mad cow disease, in the United Kingdom. Mad cow disease is a chronic[44], degenerative[45] disorder that affects the central nervous system of cattle. The disease, known as scrapie in sheep, had existed for hundreds of years without infecting other species. It only crossed over to cattle when British farmers started feeding infected sheep byproducts to their herds in the 1980s. Once BSE jumped to cows it started spreading rapidly, with 182,745 documented cases occurring between 1986 and 2002 in the United Kingdom. In response to the outbreak, European countries banned all imports of British cattle. But BSE has nonetheless been found in Europe, Canada, and the United States since then. It has also jumped to people, and a new human variant of the illness, known as Creutzfeldt-Jakob disease, is believed to be responsible for 150 deaths since 1995.

---

[41] poacher: someone who hunts illegally
[42] ravenous: greedy
[43] antibiotic: a chemical substance that destroys bacteria, such as penicillin
[44] chronic: referring to an illness that lasts for a long period of time
[45] degenerative: leading to gradual destruction of bodily structure and function

Thinking Beyond the Content

Rising to the Occasion

14 As many of these examples suggest, preventing or controlling future outbreaks of animal-borne diseases and mitigating[46] their impact will require a far broader approach than has so far been attempted by the generally isolated health systems of highly developed countries. Too often, the global response to new pathogens has been driven by fear, which has only magnified the economic and other costs of disease control.

15 That said, a few brave individuals have already begun the process of creating a new international and interdisciplinary approach to disease control. Working in some of the most remote[47] places on earth, they have slowly established knowledge-sharing networks, such as the World Conservation Union's Veterinary Specialist Group. And their contributions have already been significant. For example, when avian influenza first appeared, much attention was mistakenly directed at controlling its spread among wild birds in Northeast and Southeast Asia. It was these new informal participants in health discussions—such as conservation biologists and veterinarians working with the Wildlife Conservation Society in Cambodia and linked to staff at the Food and Agriculture Organization—who were the first to point out that the migratory routes and timing of wild birds did not actually correspond with the spread of the disease and that domestic birds were more likely the culprit. Without this insight, valuable resources would have been wasted trying to control the disease among the wrong animal population.

16 As important as such contributions have been, however, many individuals trying to develop a new global approach to health care work for nongovernmental organizations or for local governments lack the resources and a larger, formal network that could fill in the gaps in health care as it relates to wildlife and humanity. Were their resources improved, the results would be enormously beneficial; building bridges across disciplines to solve health problems can have simple but profound effects.

17 For example, studies in South America have shown that, contrary to common opinion, livestock diseases pose many more threats to wildlife than the other way around. In much of the world, reducing disease in domestic animals would benefit several industries, improve human health and livelihoods[48], and help safeguard wild animals. As this suggests, strategically increasing protections in one area of health care can benefit another. For example, gorillas and chimpanzees in central Africa have little to no immunity[49] to common human diseases, and so they are endangered by contact with local people and tourists. This risk could be dramatically reduced by implementing good preventive health programs and practices in local villages, which would benefit both people and wildlife. Already, work with the Ebola virus in gorillas and chimpanzees has

---

[46] mitigating: reducing the harm or seriousness
[47] remote: far away and isolated
[48] livelihood: a job or type of work that provides a source of income to live from
[49] immunity: resistance to a disease

shown that investments in wildlife health can protect urban human populations; in Africa, animal health workers detected the presence of Ebola in wildlife months before the first human cases occurred, providing critical lead-time to warn villagers not to hunt or handle the animals that were a source of the infection. Such a broad, "one health" approach to disease can be much more effective and inexpensive than the traditional "quarantine[50] and stamping out" strategy for fighting an illness after an outbreak has already begun. Specialists in human and animal health, in conjunction with wildlife conservation professionals, have already developed a set of guiding concepts on these themes, called the Manhattan Principles. But the ideas still need much broader acceptance to be more effective.

18   To further improve the chances of heading off and limiting the effect of animal-related diseases, a number of additional steps are necessary. To begin with, better worldwide surveillance[51] to detect infectious diseases among wildlife is needed to improve response time and reduce the costs of new outbreaks. Such surveillance differs from traditional hypothesis-driven disease research because it involves very broad searching rather than attempts to answer a highly focused question. Investment in gathering advance information can pay off handsomely; early warning of how diseases work and of their normal characteristics among animals can help limit the damage when the illnesses start to spread.

19   The World Trade Organization and other appropriate international bodies must also start requiring governments to better regulate the health aspects of international trade in wild and domestic animals. Individual states also need to implement new laws to prevent the spread of diseases within their borders. There is now plenty of evidence to suggest that human trade and consumption of wildlife have led to global health disasters; governments must therefore immediately start making serious efforts both to reduce and to regulate properly the trade of such animals internationally, regionally, and even locally.

20   On the health care side, decisions still tend to be made without sufficient input from all appropriate stakeholders[52]. For example, the decision of a Southeast Asian government in 2004 to control avian influenza by culling[53] wild migratory birds failed to identify the real source of the problem (domestic livestock) or to recognize that the wild birds were protected by at least two separate international conventions[54]. Involving experts in public health, agriculture, and environmental conservation, as well as legal counsel, in such decisions would help governments avoid repeating these mistakes and adopt more sound strategies in the future.

---

[50] quarantine: isolating a person or animal that has been exposed to a disease
[51] surveillance: observation
[52] stakeholder: someone with a personal or economic interest
[53] culling: removal of sick animal or bird from a group
[54] convention: a formal agreement

Thinking Beyond the Content

21   Finally, greater bilateral and multilateral aid is needed for efforts to gather, evaluate, and share information on infectious diseases that affect the wide range of living organisms present around the world. Too often, health experts focus on human health and agriculture alone, missing a huge part of the picture. More money must be spent on initiatives that include wildlife health and conservation in discussions of human health care; more money would also help stimulate the development of holistic efforts in areas of the world where they are most critically needed.

22   The obstacles to identifying, understanding, and sharing information about all infectious diseases on the planet may appear daunting. But they are no excuse for not trying. New, holistic approaches should be started at local and regional levels; such efforts are already proving efficient and cost-effective and are advertising the benefits of the new paradigm. Such small- and medium-scale efforts can be built up over time and run in parallel with higher-order, global coordination.

23   The time to launch such initiatives is now, before the next global pandemic[55] occurs. Bridges must be built between different scientific disciplines, and trade in wildlife must be dramatically reduced and, like the livestock industry, properly regulated. Global health will not be achieved without a philosophical shift from the expert-controlled, top-down paradigm that still dominates both science and medicine. A broader, more democratic approach is needed, one based on the understanding that there is only one world—and only one health.

---

[55] pandemic: a widespread epidemic or a fast-spreading disease that affects people in many countries

Getting at the Matter

Answer the questions in writing. Then discuss your responses with one or more partners.

1. In the opening two paragraphs, Karesh and Cook propose the main claim (thesis) of an argument. What is their claim?

2. What do the author's have to say about the basic nature of infectious disease, and what implications does this have for global trade policies?

3. Which diseases having human-animal links do the authors discuss in this article? Create a table that summarizes the animal links, geographical origins, and mode of transmission for each disease mentioned in the article. Here is an example of what your table might look like. Add additional rows for other diseases.

Disease	Animal Link	Transmission	Origin
Avian flu (H5N1 type A)	Birds	not mentioned, but generally thought to be linked to handling of infected birds	not stated, but often cited as endemic in China

4. Identify the general trends related to global trade that make animal to human transmission of disease a serious global health problem.

5. Animal disease specialists working in the field have identified a number of misconceptions regarding the transmission of diseases among animal populations. Explain several of these misconceptions.

6. What measures do Karesh and Cook propose to prevent and control global outbreaks of animal-borne diseases?

Thinking Beyond the Content

Academic Vocabulary Focus

Following are 16 words from the AWL that appear in "The Human-Animal Link." Match these words with their corresponding definitions or synonyms. Use the paragraph numbers (in parentheses) to locate the word (or the form it takes) in the reading. Use a dictionary only if necessary.

Vocabulary

_____ 1. *beneficial* (Par. 16)

_____ 2. *confirm* (Par. 7)

_____ 3. *conventions* (Par. 20)

_____ 4. *domestic* (Par. 7, 10, 11)

_____ 5. *dominate* (Par. 23)

_____ 6. *evaluate* (Par. 21)

_____ 7. *intervention* (Par. 1)

_____ 8. *isolate* (Par. 14)

_____ 9. *link* (Par. 8, 15)

_____ 10. *persist* (Par. 1)

_____ 11. *pose* (Par. 17)

_____ 12. *integrate* (Par. 2, 4)

_____ 13. *projection* (Par. 12)

_____ 14. *shift* (Par. 23)

_____ 15. *sufficient* (Par. 20)

_____ 16. *sustainable* (Par. 2)

Definition/Synonym

a. living closely with humans

b. assess, determine the value of something

c. separate from others

d. continue on, persevere

e. enough

f. prediction

g. control; have a preeminent position

h. change, move

i. agreed upon ways of doing something

j. action taken to change a result

k. verify, make certain

l. able to be maintained

m. present or cause

n. connect

o. join parts to form a whole

p. good for personal or social well-being

For Discussion

Discuss the questions with a partner or small group.

1. Of the diseases discussed in the reading, are there any that you are or have been concerned about? Explain your concerns.

2. Do you take any health-related precautions when you travel internationally? If so, describe these precautions.

Reading 3

Pre-Reading

Before reading the selection, work on these tasks with a partner or small group. What differences might you expect in the health status of adolescents living in the developing countries of the world as opposed to those living in the developed countries? List any diseases or health-related problems that you might expect among adolescents in each place.

Diseases and Health-Related Problems	
Developed Countries	**Developing Countries**

Thinking Beyond the Content

READING 3: On Being an Adolescent in the 21st Century

Paul F. A. Van Look

Excerpt from Van Look, P.F.A. (2003). On being an adolescent in the 21st century. In S. Bott, S. Jejeebhoy, I. Shah, & C. Puri (Eds.), Towards adulthood: Exploring the sexual and reproductive health of adolescents in South Asia *(pp. 31–42). Geneva, Switzerland: World Health Organization.*

Paul F. A. Van Look is the Director of Reproductive Health and Research at the World Health Organization, an agency within the United Nations that oversees international public health. Van Look's article is the introductory reading in a book primarily about sexual and reproductive health in South Asia. However, Van Look does not focus exclusively on South Asia in this introduction. Instead, drawing on data from a variety of sources he provides a broad overview of adolescent health issues in various countries around the world during the late 1990s and early 2000s.

As mentioned earlier, demographic data, especially from developing countries, is not always updated frequently, and readers need to be aware that conclusions based on data that are as much as 10 years old need to be treated with some caution. On the other hand, demographic trends often do not turn around very quickly, so even old demographic data can be more enlightening than no data.

Background

1   The World Health Organization defines "adolescence" as 10–19 years old, "youth" as 15–24 years old, and "young people" as 10–24 years old. Nevertheless, adolescence should be considered a phase rather than a fixed age group, with physical, psychological, social and cultural dimensions, perceived differently by different cultures. As a group, adolescents include nearly 1.2 billion people, about 85% of whom live in developing countries (United Nations, 1999; Figure 1). Behaviors formed in adolescence have lasting implications for individual and public health, and in many ways, a nation's fate lies in the strength and aspirations[56] of its youth—important reasons to invest in adolescent health and development. This presentation describes the general situation of adolescent health (exploring adolescent sexual and reproductive health in particular) and highlights some key elements of successful programs.

FIGURE 1   World Population of Adolescents, 1950–2050, Medium Fertility Scenario.

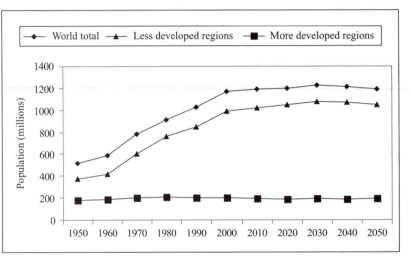

Source: United Nations (Department of Economic and Social Affairs, Population Division), (1999). *World Population Prospects. The 1998 Revision. Volume 1. Comprehensive Tables.* New York, United Nations (document ST/ESA/ SER.A/177).

The Health Status of Adolescents

2   In the absence of a single measure that can express the health status of a population in a general sense, it is difficult to assess the health of a population group. About ten years ago, researchers attempted to create such a measurement unit, called the DALY (Disability-Adjusted Life Years), in order to quantify[57] the global burden[58] of disease throughout the world (Murray & Lopez, 1996). This measure tries to capture[59] two

---

[56] aspiration: goal, desire to do an important or great thing
[57] quantify: measure
[58] burden: heavy load, something difficult to carry
[59] capture: preserve in images, words or numbers

elements at once—years of life lost due to premature mortality[60] and years of healthy life lost from disability, adjusted for severity of the disability. For example, DALYs lost due to heart attack may include years lost as a result of premature death, as well as healthy years lost due to disability such as becoming bedridden[61].

3   Researchers have used DALYs to quantify the burden of each disease in the world in specific regions and in different population groups. For example, Chris Murray and Catherine Michaud attempted to quantify the degree of ill-health in adolescents in terms of DALYs in both developing and developed regions of the world. At the global level, they found that adolescents bore nearly 10% (6.6% in developed regions) of the ill-health present in the world in 1990. We typically think of adolescence as being the prime of life—relatively free from infectious diseases of childhood and from conditions associated with ageing[62]. Thus, one would expect that the proportion of ill-health attributable to adolescents would be small. But clearly it is not the case. In 1990, most DALYs (92.0%) among adolescents were lost in developing regions, which is not surprising, since that is where most adolescents live. Adolescents in developed regions were slightly healthier in terms of DALYs than their counterparts in developing regions.

TABLE 1 Causes of DALYs (Percentage of Total) in Descending Order among Adolescents Globally, 1990 (Total DALYs in thousands 5 132,562)

Rank	Disease or Injury	Percent of total
1	Unipolar major depression	6.9
2	Road traffic accidents	4.9
3	Falls	4.0
4	Iron-deficiency anaemia	3.7
5	War	3.5
6	Lower respiratory infections	3.3
7	Drowning	2.8
8	Self-inflicted injuries	2.7
9	Alcohol use	2.3
10	Diarrhoeal diseases	2.3
	Total:	**36.3**

Source: Murray & Michaud, 1996. Unpublished data.

4   Table 1 presents the 10 most common factors that led to death and disability among adolescents globally in 1990, as measured in terms of DALYs. The worldwide list mirrors the conditions that affect developing countries, including infectious diseases, diarrheal

---

[60] premature mortality: to die early before one's time
[61] bedridden: unable to get out of bed
[62] ageing: the physical changes that accompany getting older

diseases, iron-deficiency anemia, accidents, injuries, war, and suicide attempts. Perhaps surprisingly, the top ranked condition is a mental health problem—unipolar major depression. Altogether the top ten conditions represent more than one-third of DALYs lost among adolescents worldwide (Table 1).

5   Looking at developed and developing regions separately, factors leading to death or disability in developing regions are the same as for the world as a whole, but the pattern is quite different in developed regions. Only three factors appear on both lists. Instead of infectious diseases and anaemia that are prominent[63] in developing regions, the list for developed regions includes several other mental health problems, such as bipolar

TABLE 2   Causes of DALYs (Percentage of Total) in Descending Order among Adolescents in Developing and Developed Regions, 1990

Developing Regions			Developed Regions		
Rank	Disease or injury	% of total	Rank	Disease or injury	% of total
1	Unipolar major depression	6.5	1	Road traffic accidents	12.3
2	Road traffic accidents	4.2	2	Unipolar major depression	11.3
3	Falls	4.2	3	Alcohol use	8.3
4	Iron-deficiency anaemia	3.9	4	Schizophrenia	4.4
5	War	3.6	5	Drug use	3.5
6	Lower respiratory infections	3.5	6	Bipolar disorder	3.4
7	Drowning	2.9	7	Obsessive-compulsive disorders	3.3
8	Self-inflicted injuries	2.7	8	Asthma	2.6
9	Diarrhoeal diseases	2.4	9	Osteoarthritis	2.5
10	Malaria	2.2	10	Self-inflicted injuries	2.3
	Total:	**36.3**		**Total:**	**54.0**
	Total DALYs in thousands = 121,927			Total DALYs in thousands = 10,635	

Source: Murray & Michaud, 1996. Unpublished data.

---

[63] prominent: obvious, easy to observe

Thinking Beyond the Content

disorders, obsessive-compulsive disorders[64] (which include, for instance, anorexia[65] and bulimia[66]) and schizophrenia[67]. Drugs and alcohol use, which are often associated with mental health disorders, are also high on the list. Altogether, the top ten factors represent more than 50% of the total amount of DALYs lost among adolescents in developed regions (Table 2).

6   One major limitation of using DALYs to measure ill-health among adolescents is that DALYs only capture those problems that are manifest[68] at that moment in time. However, many events and behaviors that begin during adolescence lead to serious problems later in life. Substance abuse patterns, such as smoking and drinking, often develop in adolescence but do not cause ill-health until adulthood. For example, young people who start drinking before age 15 are four times more likely to become alcoholics than those who start at age 21 or later, and most adults who smoke began during adolescence (World Health Organization, 2001).

7   The Bulletin of the World Health Organization recently published the results of the Global Youth Tobacco Survey (Warren et al., 2000). Researchers concluded that in spite of efforts to counter it, tobacco use among children and adolescents is increasing, and the average age of initiating smoking is declining. In many countries,

FIGURE 2   Percentage of Students Aged 13–15 Years Smoking Cigarettes (Global Youth Tobacco Survey, 1999).

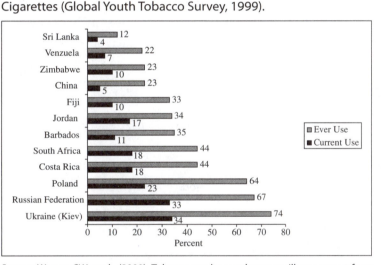

Source: Warren CW et al., (2000). Tobacco use by youth: a surveillance report from the Global Youth Tobacco Survey project. Bulletin of the World Health Organization, 78(7): 868–876.

---

[64] obsessive-compulsive disorder: a serious mental illness characterized by recurring thoughts (obsessions) and repetitive behaviors (compulsions)

[65] anorexia: an eating disorder in which the subject excessively diets to the point of serious ill-health or death

[66] bulimia: an eating disorder in which the subject experiences periods of overeating (binging) followed by under eating, use of laxatives, or self-induced vomiting (purging) to lose weight

[67] schizophrenia: a serious mental illness in which a person's thoughts and feelings are not based on what is really happening

[68] manifest: observable

between one-third and three-fourths of 13–15 year olds have smoked cigarettes, and around 20–35% of these young people are current users (Figure 2). Once children and adolescents start smoking cigarettes, it becomes extremely difficult for them to stop, even when they have a strong desire to do so. The survey found that a large majority (between 60% and 80%) of 13–15 year-olds who smoke expressed a desire to quit the habit. The percent who have been unsuccessful was nearly equally high (50–70%). If these trends continue, tobacco will kill 250 million people who are children or adolescents today.

Adolescent Sexual and Reproductive Health

8   Though early marriage continues to be the norm in some areas, age-at marriage among both sexes is rising in virtually every country of the world.

9   Age at first sexual activity has not followed this trend, however, and in many areas tends to begin at a younger age than in the past. As a result, there is a growing window of opportunity for premarital[69] sexual activity. A recent report by the Population Reference Bureau (2000) compares the median age at marriage (both formal marriage and cohabitation[70]) and the median age at first intercourse. As Table 3 illustrates, a large proportion of adolescents experience first intercourse before marriage in all countries listed. In other words, the evidence clearly indicates that a large proportion of adolescents— if not the majority—are engaging in premarital sexual activity.

TABLE 3   Age at Marriage and Age at First Sexual Intercourse among Young Women*— Selected Countries

Country	Median Age at Marriage**	Median Age at First Intercourse
Cameroon	18.0	15.9
Kenya	20.2	16.8
Niger	15.3	15.3
Bolivia	20.9	19.0
Brazil	21.0	18.8
Guatemala	19.2	18.6
Haiti	20.5	18.7
Indonesia	19.9	19.8
Philippines	22.7	22.8

*Among women interviewed when 25–29 years old.
**Includes formal marriage and cohabitation.
Source: Population Reference Bureau, (2000). *The World's Youth 2000*. Washington, DC. Population Reference Bureau.

[69] premarital: before marriage
[70] cohabitation: living together

Thinking Beyond the Content

10 Aggregate data often hide important differences between subgroups, including differences between the sexes. Over the past decade, WHO has supported a series of studies involving young people, which have shed light on these differences. Data extracted from 29 of these studies (Brown et al., 2001) indicate that a higher proportion of boys than girls report having engaged in premarital sex in nearly all countries. In some countries, that proportion is as high as 70% among boys, whereas among girls it tends to be below 40% (Figure 3).

FIGURE 3 Proportion of Young People Reporting Premarital Sexual Activity During the 1990s—Selected Studies.

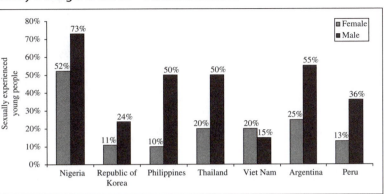

*Note: The studies were not designed to be similar. Hence the samples, methodologies, and age ranges varied.
Source: Brown, A., et al., (2001). *Sexual relations among young people in developing countries. Evidence from WHO case studies.* Geneva, World Health Organization (WHO/RHR/01.8).

FIGURE 4 Proportion of Young People Reporting Two or More Sexual Partners—Selected Studies.

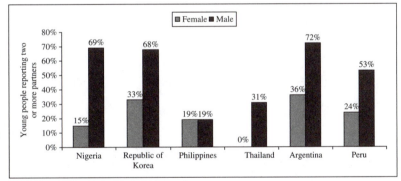

Source: Brown, A., et al., (2001). *Sexual relations among young people in developing countries. Evidence from WHO case studies.* Geneva World Health Organization (WHO/RHR/01.8).

11 While part of this difference may be due to the tendency of males to over-report and females to under-report premarital sexual activity, much of this difference seems to be genuine, reflecting gender-related double standards[71].

12 These studies suggest other important differences between the sexes in terms of numbers and types of partners. For example, boys tend to report more sexual partners than girls in all countries (Figure 4).

13 In the majority of cases, girls reported having first sexual intercourse[72] with a boyfriend or fiancé, and only rarely with casual partners[73]. Boys, on the other hand,

---

[71] double standard: when a standard is applied more leniently to one group than to another
[72] intercourse: sexual contact or union
[73] casual partners: persons met by chance

reported a greater diversity of types of first partners. Around 60% of boys reported that fiancées were their first partner, but a large proportion of boys had sexual partners who were commercial sex workers (Figure 5). **14** These studies also found that a high proportion of girls reported coercive[74] sexual experiences, in some cases as many as 40%. Boys also reported coercive experiences, but did so much less frequently (Figure 6). This collection of studies suggests that premarital sexual intercourse is often not premeditated[75] and happens at the spur of the moment[76]. Contra-

FIGURE 5 Type of Sexual Partner at Debut, or Currently, by Sex—Selected Studies.

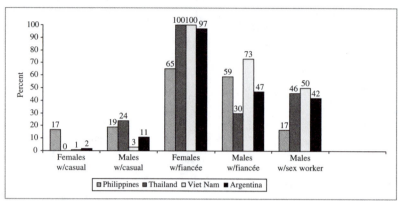

Source: Brown, A., et al., (2001). *Sexual relations among young people in developing countries: Evidence from WHO case studies.* Geneva World Health Organization (WHO/RHR/01.8).

FIGURE 6 Proportion of Young People Reporting a Coercive Sexual Experience—Selected Studies.

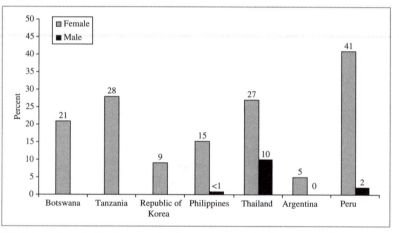

NB: Data not available for males in three countries. Studies measured coercion in different ways. For example, data from Argentina refer only to "rape."
Source: Brown, A., et al., (2001). *Sexual relations among young people in developing countries: Evidence from WHO case studies.* Geneva, World Health Organization (WHO/RHR/01.8).

ception is rarely and irregularly used at sexual debut[77]. After sexual initiation, the pattern

---

[74] coercive: make someone do something they do not want to do
[75] premeditated: planned
[76] spur of the moment: spontaneously, without planning
[77] sexual debut: first sexual experience

Thinking Beyond the Content

of adolescent sexual behavior is often erratic[78], and few young people report consistent and correct use of contraception. **15** Using data from Demographic and Health Surveys, the Population Reference Bureau recently analyzed contraceptive use among single, sexually

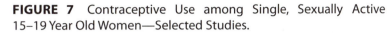

FIGURE 7 Contraceptive Use among Single, Sexually Active 15–19 Year Old Women—Selected Studies.

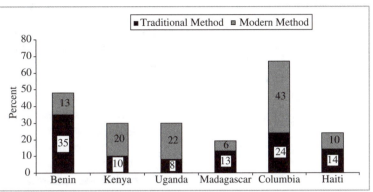

Source: Population Reference Bureau, (2000). *The World's Youth 2000*. Washington, DC, Population Reference Bureau.

active 16–19 year-old women in a number of countries (Population Reference Bureau, 2000). Their analysis found that many single, young, sexually active women do not use contraception, and a high proportion of those who do, use less effective, traditional methods (Figure 7). Over 14 million adolescents give birth each year, and about 85% of those births occur in developing countries (Alan Guttmacher Institute, 1998; Figure 8). Adolescent pregnancies and births carry higher risks—for both the mother and the newborn—than births and pregnancies among older women. The maternal mortality rate among this age group is twice as high as for women in their 20s, and more adolescent girls aged 15–19 die from pregnancy related causes than from any other cause (United Nations Children's Fund, 1998). In addition, the risk of death during the first year of life is

FIGURE 8 Births to Adolescent Women Each Year in Millions, by Region (Total 14 Millions).

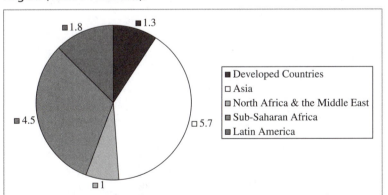

Source: Alan Guttmacher Institute, (1998). *Into a New World: Young Women's Sexual and Reproductive Lives*. New York, Alan Guttmacher Institute.

---

[78] erratic: irregular, prone to error

1.5 times higher for infants born to mothers before the age of 20 than for infants born to women in the third decade of their life (Population Reference Bureau, 2000).

16 Data compiled by the Alan Guttmacher Institute suggest that between 33% and 66% of births among teenagers are unplanned in most countries (Figure 9).

17 Many adolescents who experience an unplanned pregnancy resort to abortion—often under unsafe conditions, or late in pregnancy when abortions carry higher risk. Evidence suggests that adolescents have abortions in high numbers, irrespective of the type of abortion laws that exist in a country (Alan Guttmacher Institute, 1998). For example, high numbers of abortions occur in countries with very restrictive abortion laws, such as the Dominican Republic, as well as in countries with less restrictive laws such as the United States of America (Figure 10).

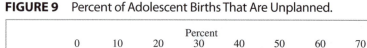

FIGURE 9   Percent of Adolescent Births That Are Unplanned.

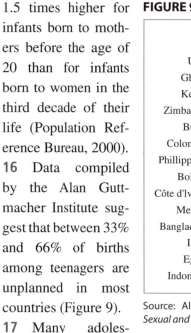

Source: Alan Guttmacher Institute, (1998). *Into a New World: Young Women's Sexual and Reproductive Lives.* New York, Alan Guttmacher Institute.

FIGURE 10   Number of Abortions Per 100 Adolescent Women Aged 15–19, Selected Studies.

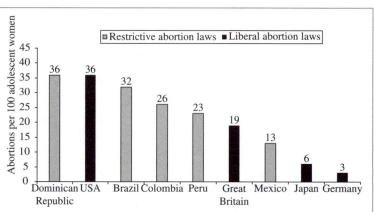

Source: Alan Guttmacher Institute, (1998). *Into a New World: Young Women's Sexual and Reproductive Lives.* New York, Alan Guttmacher Institute.

Thinking Beyond the Content

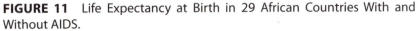

FIGURE 11 Life Expectancy at Birth in 29 African Countries With and Without AIDS.

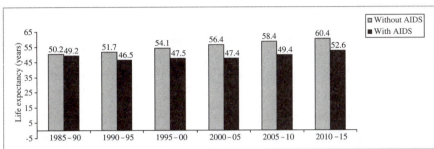

Source: United Nations (Department of Economic and Social Affairs, Population Division), (2000). *World Population Prospects. The 1998 Revision. Volume 3, Analytical Report.* New York, United Nations (document ST/ESA/SER.A/186).

18 Other important consequences of unprotected intercourse include sexually transmitted infections (STIs). Here again, for biological and social reasons, adolescents are at a high risk. Out of an estimated 340 million cases of curable STIs in the world, at least one-third occur in young people under age 25. This means that more than one out of 20 adolescents contracts a curable STI each year. In addition to curable STIs, many cases of STIs occur for which no cure exists—foremost among them HIV infection. According to estimates, half of all new HIV infections currently occur among 15–24 year-olds, the equivalent of 2.5 million new infections each year (Joint United Nations Program on HIV/AIDS, 2001).

19 To demonstrate what might have happened in sub- Saharan Africa if HIV/AIDS did not exist, Figure 11 illustrates the HIV/AIDS pandemic's impact on projected life expectancy in 29 African countries. Without HIV/AIDS, life expectancy should have increased over time. Instead, since the emergence of HIV/AIDS, life expectancy has decreased in these countries. According to some estimates there will be a difference of nine years between what it would have been with and without HIV/AIDS by 2010–2015 (United Nations, 2000). In terms of life expectancy, HIV/AIDS has wiped out decades of work of eradicating[79] infectious diseases and improving health systems in the space of ten years (Figure 11).

20 Despite the burden of sexual and reproductive ill health among adolescents in the world today, there are many reasons to be optimistic about adolescents' health and well-being. First, more people are gaining access to information as a result of increased exposure to mass media. Levels of education are rising among girls and boys in virtually every country, and evidence suggests that educated people are better able to look after their own health (The World Bank, 1993). In addition, declining levels of early marriage in nearly all countries should positively influence maternal and newborn health, provided that young unmarried people have access to appropriate reproductive health services,

---

[79] eradicate: get rid of, eliminate

particularly contraceptive services. Use of contraceptives by adolescents is increasing (Population Reference Bureau, 2001), and this may lead to fewer unplanned pregnancies; increased condom use should also lower rates of STI infection. Finally, there have even been positive results in the area of HIV/AIDS. For example, as a result of prevention efforts, HIV prevalence in Uganda has gradually declined among 13–19 year old girls from about 4.5% to 1.5% since the beginning of the 1990s (Joint United Nations Program on HIV/AIDS, 2000; Figure 12).

21 Similarly, in Zambia, intensive prevention efforts have helped bring down HIV levels among young women attending antenatal clinics. Various clinics in Lusaka reported levels of HIV infection higher than 25% in 1993. These levels have since dropped below 17%, demonstrating that it is possible to influence trends in HIV prevalence (Joint United Nations Program on HIV/AIDS, 2000; Figure 13).

FIGURE 12 HIV Prevalence Rate among 13–19 Year-olds, Masaka, Uganda, 1989–1997.

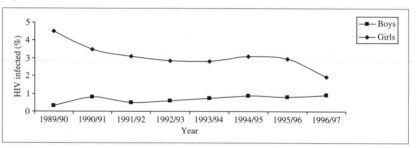

Source: Joint United Nations Programme on HIV/AIDS, (2000). *Report on the Global HIV/AIDS Epidemic, June 2000.* Geneva, UNAIDS.

FIGURE 13 HIV Prevalence Rate among Pregnant 15–19 Year-Olds, Lusaka, Zambia, 1993–1998.

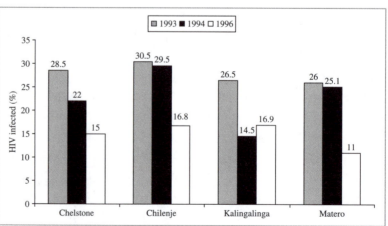

Source: Joint United Nations Programme on HIV/AIDS, (2000). *Report on the Global HIV/ AIDS Epidemic, June 2000.* Geneva, UNAIDS.

Thinking Beyond the Content

Conclusions: Key Elements of Successful Programs

22   In 1999, Dr. Gro Harlem Brundtland, Director General of WHO, addressed the ICPD + 5[80] in The Hague. During her address, she argued that "there is a deep-seated discomfort when dealing with adolescent sexuality. We need to change this." As researchers, policy-makers and program managers address adolescent sexuality and search for ways to improve young people's lives, they should consider a number of elements that seem to be key to successful programs. First, adolescents themselves need to participate in program planning and design. Second, programs need to address health problems in a comprehensive manner. Many problems that adolescents experience have common roots and common determinants[81]. It makes little sense to address one particular health problem while ignoring others.

23   In addition, programs should combine interventions from different areas, such as health, education and life skills development, micro-credit, small business development and safe environments for entertainment. Whenever possible, programs should build links with existing services in order to achieve cost-effectiveness and avoid duplication. To reinforce services, ways need to be found to provide young people with more supportive environments within their families, schools and communities.

24   All these recommendations require strong program management. It is not easy to develop comprehensive programs for adolescents that are able to deal with many facets of adolescent life. To meet the needs of different categories of adolescents in ways that respect cultural diversity requires great skill from service providers and program managers.

25   The above recommendations have emerged from lessons learned or current thinking about programming for young people, but more work is needed to define the elements of successful programs on the basis of empirical evidence.

---

[80] ICPD + 5: refers to the special session of the International Conference on Population and Development held five years after the initial conference that was held in 1994 by the UN General Assembly dealing with global health issues

[81] determinants: causes

REFERENCES

Alan Guttmacher Institute. (1998). *Into a new world: Young women's sexual and reproductive lives.* New York: Alan Guttmacher Institute.

Brown, A., Jejeebhoy, S. J., Shah I., & Yount, K. M. (2001). *Sexual relations among young people in developing countries: Evidence from WHO case studies.* Geneva: World Health Organization (WHO/ RHR/01.8).

Joint United Nations Program on HIV/AIDS. (2000). *Report on the global HIV/AIDS epidemic, June 2000.* Geneva: UNAIDS.

Joint United Nations Program on HIV/AIDS. (2001). *Children and young people in the world of AIDS.* Geneva: UNAIDS.

Murray, C. J .L., & Lopez, A. D. (Eds.). (1996). *The global burden of disease: A comprehensive assessment of mortality and disability from diseases, injuries and risk factors in 1990 and projected to 2020. Global burden of disease and injury series: Vol. 1.* Cambridge, MA: Harvard School of Public Health on behalf of the World Health Organization and the World Bank.`

Murray, C. J. L., Michaud, C. (1996). *Recalculation of DALYs according to age groups pertaining to adolescents, youth, and young people—Description of methodology and data used for calculation* (unpublished paper).

Population Reference Bureau. (2000). *The world's youth 2000.* Washington, DC: Population Reference Bureau.

———. *Youth in Sub-Saharan Africa: A chartbook on sexual experience and reproductive health.* Washington, DC: Population Reference Bureau.

United Nations (Department of Economic and Social Affairs, Population Division). (1999). *World population prospects. The 1998 revision. Vol. 1: Comprehensive tables.* New York: United Nations (ST/ESA/SER.A/177).

———. *World population prospects. The 1998 revision. Vol. 3: Analytical report.* New York: United Nations (ST/ESA/SER.A/186).

United Nations Children's Fund. (1998). *Progress of nations 1998.* New York: UNICEF.

Warren, C. W. et al. (2000). Tobacco use by youth: a surveillance report from the Global Youth Tobacco Survey Project. *Bulletin of the World Health Organization, 78*(7), 868–876.

The World Bank. (1993). *World development report 1993—Investing in health.* Oxford: Oxford University Press on behalf of the World Bank.

World Health Organization. (2001). Briefing note 3 on adolescent health—Provision of health services. *Briefing notes on selected adolescent health issues.* Geneva: World Health Organization, Department of Child and Adolescent Health and Development.

Critical Focus Review

Review several previous Critical Focus skills by completing the following tasks.

1. The first reading of this unit, "Global Trends in Tobacco Use," included several graphs and a table, and you learned a systematic way of describing and explaining the information in a graph. The third reading, "On Being an Adolescent in the 21st Century," also makes use of many graphs. Form a group with two or three other classmates, select several graphs from the reading, and take turns describing and explaining one of the graphs to the other members of your group.

2. In addition to graphs, "On Being an Adolescent in the 21st Century" has a reference list and many in-text citations. In Unit 1, you learned about citations and references and began paying greater attention to them. You learned how to read them, and you learned that a critical reader can use them to identify information that he or she might want to explore in more detail. Using the citations from "On Being an Adolescent in the 21st Century," indicate in the chart the issues discussed in the reading along with the associated in-text citation and the title of the source. Some of the information has been provided to get you started.

Issue	Citation	Source
What is a DALY (disability adjusted life year)? How is it measured?	*(Murray & Lopez, 1996)*	The Global Burden of Disease
Adolescent tobacco use		
	(Population Reference Bureau, 2000) (Brown et al., 2001)	The World's Youth
Contraceptive use among adolescents		
Teen pregnancy rates		
	(United Nations Children's Fund, 1998)	
	(Alan Guttmacher Institute, 1998)	

Thinking Beyond the Content

Getting at the Matter

Answer the questions in writing. Then discuss your responses with one or more partners.

1. Briefly explain the concept of the DALY. What does it stand for? In what way is it useful? What is its disadvantage as a measure of ill health?

2. Compare and contrast the health problems of adolescents living in the developing world with that of adolescents living in the developed world.

3. Compare and contrast the differences between adolescent males and adolescent females with regard to sexual activity. The article suggests it may be difficult for health workers to get accurate information on the sexual activity of males and females. Why?

4. Summarize the health risks to adolescents associated with sexual activity. In what way(s) are the health risks for adolescent females different than for adolescent males?

Academic Vocabulary Focus

Some words may have more than one meaning; therefore, dictionaries usually provide multiple definitions for a word. For this reason, it is important to find the correct definition when using a dictionary. The 16 words in this exercise are some of the words from the AWL that appear in the reading "Being an Adolescent in the 21st Century. Review how the words are used in the text, and then choose the one definition that most closely defines how the word is used in the text. Once you are done, compare your answers with those of another student.

Academic Word List Vocabulary			
access	adjusted	aggregate	comprehensive
consequences	consistent	dimensions	elements
emergence	empirical	equivalent	illustrates
instance	invest	norm	prime

1. *access* (Paragraph 19)
   a. entry or approach
   b. opportunity for use

2. *adjusted* (Paragraph 2)
   a. adapted to a new circumstance
   b. changed slightly

3. *aggregate* (Paragraph 10)
   a. forming a total
   b. resembling a rock

4. *comprehensive* (Paragraph 21)
   a. covering many eventualities
   b. including all

5. *consequences* (Paragraph 17)
   a. logical conclusions
   b. results

6. *consistent* (Paragraph 13)
   a. reliable
   b. with common solutions

7. *dimensions* (Paragraph 1)
   a. aspects
   b. sizes

8. *elements* (Paragraph 1)
   a. a basic unit of matter
   b. a separate or identifiable part of something

9. *emergence* (Paragraph 18)
   a. the act of appearing
   b. appearance in adult form

10. *empirical* (Paragraph 24)
    a. based on or characterized by observation and experiment rather than theory
    b. based on practical experience rather than on applied theory or scientific proof

11. *equivalent* (Paragraph 17)
    a. with the same solution
    b. equal to

12. *illustrates* (Paragraph 9)
    a. fully demonstrates or explains
    b. to be characteristic of something

13. *instance* (Paragraph 5)
    a. an example of a particular situation or event
    b. an occurrence of something

14. *invest* (Paragraph 1)
    a. to contribute effort to something
    b. to use money to buy or participate in an endeavor

15. *norm* (Paragraph 8)
    a. a required level of achievement
    b. a standard pattern of behavior that is considered normal in a particular society

16. *prime* (Paragraph 3)
    a. the best state or stage of something
    b. the earliest part of something

For Discussion

Choose one of the topics (A or B) to discuss in groups.

A. There is a saying that "today's children are our future." In the first section of the reading, the author lists ten health issues that commonly affect adolescents.

1. Look back at Table 2 (page 112). Are any of these issues a concern in your country? Can you think of any other health issues that you think should be on the list?

2. What do you think is the most important action the government or public health system in your country should do to ensure that the youth of today grow up to be healthy and strong?

B. Fill out this survey and discuss your opinions with the other members of your group.

Agree	Disagree	
		1. In my culture, most parents feel comfortable giving their children information related to sex and reproduction.
		2. My parents have always felt comfortable talking about sex.
		3. I first learned about sex from my father/mother.
		4. I first learned about sex from someone outside of my family.
		5. In my culture, sex education is taught in school.
		6. In my culture, it is important for adolescents to learn about contraceptive methods.
		7. In my culture, it is expected that a young person will wait until marriage before having sex for the first time.
		8. Most young people in my culture do not have sex before marriage.
		9. Teaching young people about contraceptive methods encourages them to experiment with sex.
		10. In order to combat the global AIDS epidemic, it is essential for condoms to be widely available.

For Further Investigaton

1. Find the website of the World Health Organization (WHO). What health topics are currently being presented on the WHO homepage?

2. Select a topic from the WHO list of health topics, and find out more about the global status of that particular issue.

3. Select a country from the WHO list, and find out more about the particular health concerns faced by that country. You might find it interesting to compare a developing country with a developed country.

4. Tobacco companies have faced lawsuits and increasing criticism for their continued marketing of tobacco. At the same time, many companies have mounted information campaigns that seem to be aimed at discouraging young people from taking up smoking. Health educators and anti-smoking groups tend to view these campaigns with distrust, arguing that the tobacco industry is merely trying to protect its public image, while continuing to keep a spotlight on images of smoking. Investigate one of these aspects of this debate:

    a. techniques used by tobacco advertisers to promote smoking
    b. suggestions for resisting tobacco advertising
    c. analysis of the anti-smoking rhetoric coming from tobacco companies

5. Try to find the most recent data that estimates global rates of tobacco use. Do the generalizations made in Reading 1 continue to hold today, or is the situation significantly different?

6. Investigate global measures or measures being taken by a specific country to control tobacco use.

7. Using WHO resources or sources from an academic library, research the health problems of adolescents. Survey the range of problems facing adolescents, and choose a specific problem to focus on in more detail. You might find it necessary to restrict your focus to a specific problem in a specific country or region. Or you might compare the extent of a particular problem in two different countries.

4: Thinking about Sport

Sports are immensely popular in many modern societies. Sports fans include not only people with a passion for participating in sports, but also those with a passion for watching others participate, otherwise known as sports fans or spectators. Spectator sports are also big business, generating billions of dollars of revenue. Moreover, sport is a popular topic for small talk[1]. But perhaps you have never thought of sport as a topic for serious academic discussion. The readings in this unit deal with sport from three points of view: sociological, anthropological, and psychological.

The first reading, "Sport: Work or Play," is a critical analysis by sport sociologist Allen Sack of historical attempts by scholars to define the concept of sport. After evaluating these attempts, Sack proposes a definition that he hopes is an improvement over earlier definitions.

The second reading, "The Meaning of Sport," is an excerpt from the introduction to a book on anthropology of sport. In this reading, the author observes that while sport sociologists have devoted much effort to defining the concept, anthropologists are likely to find these definitions inadequate, especially when they try to apply them across cultures.

---

[1] small talk: light informal conversation engaged in mainly as a way to socialize

In the final reading, "Why Competition Excites Us," sociologist Ellis Cashmore explains the human fascination with sports as a way of compensating for a modern lifestyle that has become too comfortable and secure. According to this view, sport is the way humans exercise instinctual abilities which civilized life has made unnecessary.

Reading 1

In this reading, sociologist Allen Sack takes up the challenge of trying to construct a clear definition of sport that can avoid ambiguity and withstand critical scrutiny. However, before reading Sack's article, it will be helpful to be familiar with an important critical-thinking strategy.

Critical Focus: Constructing and Testing Definitions

The ability to construct and test definitions is fundamental to critical thinking. In your daily—non-academic—life, you may be satisfied with what you think are the commonly agreed-upon meanings of everyday words. You may talk with a friend about sport and never question whether you and your friend truly share the same concept of sport. However, academic writers have to be more precise. They have to define their disciplines, and they have to clearly communicate the meanings of various terms within their disciplines. One way that they do this is by creating **formal definitions.** Constructing a formal definition involves classifying a concept by placing it in a category and then distinguishing it from other members of the category by specifying its unique qualities and features.

As a concrete example, consider the concept "scissors." To formally define *scissors,* we begin by placing it in a category— "a scissors is a tool." Then we need to specify the features that distinguish it from the entire class of tools. So we try, "a scissors is a tool used for cutting various kinds of materials." Having constructed this definition, we have to test it before we can be sure that it will work. Testing a definition involves trying to think of an item that has all of the features specified in the definition but that clearly does not belong in the same family.

It is not very difficult to see problems with our definition of scissors. Knives, razor blades, and saws all have the features specified in the definition, but they are clearly not scissors. Therefore, we need to add further qualifications to our definition. We need to add that: "a scissors consists of two handles and a pair of opposing blades connected at a pivot point so that the blades can be brought together in order to slice the material that is to be cut." Successive rounds of construction and testing should eventually satisfy us that we have produced a definition that will admit all scissors and exclude all non-scissors.

This kind of thinking requires the reader to exercise some imagination. When reading material in which the writer is defining difficult or complex ideas, the critical reader should not just accept whatever definition the writer offers. The critical reader questions the definition, tries to poke holes in it, tries to find its limitations. The Pre-Reading activity that follows is designed to get you to think critically about a concept that you might currently take for granted.

Pre-Reading

Apply the strategy described in the Critical Focus on page 133 to the concept of sports. Work alone or with a partner.

1. Try to construct a formal definition of sports.

2. Test your definition by trying to think of activities that, according to your definition, should be sports but that seem clearly not to be.

3. Revise your definition until you are satisfied that it effectively excludes all non-examples of sport and includes all examples.

READING 1: Sport: Play or Work?

Allen Sack

From Sack, A. L. (1977). Sport: Play or work? In P. Stevens, Jr. (Ed.). Studies in the anthropology of play *(pp. 186–195). West Point, NY: Leisure Press.*

This article, by sociologist Allen Sack was written when sociology of sport was more or less in its youth as an academic discipline. During the 1960s and '70s, sport sociologists put a lot of effort into trying to define their field. In particular, they took up the problem of trying to define the term *sport*. As you will soon see, this is no easy task. Although numerous writers have tried, no one has been entirely successful, and for the most part, sport sociologists have moved on to other concerns. However, these attempts to define a difficult-to-define concept still make interesting reading, and this article written in 1977 by Allen Sack is a particularly well-argued attempt to define the term *sport*. Sack has a PhD in sociology and has written many scholarly papers and books on the role of sport in society. As you read, try to observe how, as a writer, he appears to apply the strategy we have explained on page 133 for constructing and testing definitions.

1　　The sociology of sport, while making some progress toward developing precise concepts, has still not adequately staked out[2] the boundaries of its field of investigation. More specifically, a review of literature reveals considerable disagreement and inconsistency concerning the concepts play, game, and sport. Some writers, like Huizinga and Caillois, treat play and games as virtually synonymous[3] terms. Likewise, Loy, by defining both games and sport as "playful" competitions comes very close to making sport a subcategory of play. Edwards, on the other hand, argues that play and sport have nothing in common and places them at opposite ends of a continuum[4]. It will be argued here that all of the above formulations[5] are inadequate because they fail to make explicit the essential difference between sport as work and sport as play. It is the relationship between sport, work, and play that will constitute the central concern of this paper.

Play and Work

2　　Many contemporary discussions of the play concept find their starting point in Johan Huizinga's classic work *Homo Ludens*. According to Huizinga, play is:

> a free activity standing quite consciously outside "ordinary" life as being "not serious," but at the same time absorbing the player intensely and utterly. It is an activity connected with no material interest, and no profit can be gained by it. It proceeds within its own proper boundaries of time and space according to fixed rules and in an orderly manner. It promotes the formation of social groupings which tend to surround themselves with secrecy and to stress their difference from the common world by disguise or other means.

3　　Although in need of considerable refinement, Huizinga's definition does nonetheless point to some of the most important features of play. First, play is a free or voluntary activity. A person plays because he enjoys it, and when he no longer finds the activity gratifying[6], he is free to stop. According to Huizinga, "play can be deferred or suspended at any time . . . it is never a task." Neither the ballplayer who attends practice for fear of losing his scholarship nor the child who is forced to participate in little league baseball can truly be said to be playing. The more one is obliged to participate in a given activity (whether one likes it or not) the less that activity resembles play.

---

[2] stake out: to mark, define, delimit
[3] synonymous: having the same meaning
[4] continuum: something that is continuous—and that can not be clearly separated from what is immediately next to it
[5] formulation: the act of clearly explaining something in a specific way
[6] gratifying: giving a sense of pleasure or satisfaction

Note: Here the author lists other writers but no other elements of a citation. In cases like this, check the end of the reading or the end of the book to see whether the cited names appear in a reference list (for example, see page 145). If no reference information is listed, try searching a library catalog or using a search engine like *scholar.google.com/*.

4 The second important characteristic of play is that it stands outside ordinary life and is not "serious." This can be interpreted to mean that play is set apart from the pragmatic[7] concerns associated with making a living. A person engages in play because it is intrinsically rewarding, not because it is a means to some end lying outside of the sphere of play itself. To quote Huizinga, "play interpolates[8] itself as a temporary activity satisfying in itself and ending there." Play is never imposed by physical necessity. Thus, it is bracketed off[9] from what one often considers to be "real" life. It should be added, and Huizinga was well aware of this, that play can proceed with the utmost seriousness within its own boundaries.

5 The sport of mountain climbing serves to illustrate the separateness of the play sphere. If a man climbs a mountain to establish a weather observatory or to train soldiers in winter survival techniques, his actions more closely resemble work than play. As climbing ceases to be an end in itself and becomes infused[10] with the concerns of the workaday world, the more the play element retreats to the background. On the other hand, if a person endures the pain associated with high altitude climbing, risks serious injury and even death, merely for the sake of climbing to the summit, this represents play in its purest form.

6 Closely related to this idea that play is separate is Huizinga's insistence that play is connected with no material interest and no profit can be gained by it. It would be more accurate to say, however, that play is pursued for no material interest or profit. In this latter form, the statement simply re-emphasizes the point that play, in its purest form is intrinsically rewarding. The more that one pursues an activity for extrinsic rewards[11], or is subject to pressures and demands emanating from outside the play world, the more the activity becomes work.

7 With regard to Huizinga's assertion that play proceeds within its own proper boundaries of time and space according to fixed rules, a few words are in order. First, in as much as all human behavior proceeds within boundaries of time and space, this quality is not particularly helpful in defining play. The question of rules is not so simple. On the one hand, one might argue that *all* social behavior is governed by rules, and that play, being social behavior, is no exception. On the other hand, those who are offended by such an oversocialized view of man would argue that man is also

---

[7] pragmatic: practical, not just theoretical
[8] interpolate: to insert
[9] bracket off: to separate from
[10] become infused: be filled with
[11] extrinsic rewards: benefits like praise or money that an individual receives from an outside source

capable of impulsive[12], unstructured, and creative activity which is freed from social conventions. Adherents to the latter position are apt to assert that play can have both its spontaneous and structured manifestations. It is important to note, however, that whichever interpretation is chosen, the existence of normative regulation per se does not preclude an activity from being play. In fact, it is precisely the challenge created by rules, freely accepted, that makes some forms of play so fascinating.

8   In summary, suffice it to say that play is characterized by its freedom, separateness, and its lack of dependence on material interest or profit. Although most play activity is governed by rules which are freely accepted by participants, some play forms, e.g., lovers frolicking in autumn leaves or children rolling recklessly down a grassy embankment, have little or possibly no normative regulation. Generally speaking, the more an activity is a task or obligation oriented to the pragmatic concerns of making a living and pursued for profit or material interest, the more it approximates work.

Games, Play, and Work

9   The concept of game is often confused with play. This is especially obvious in Caillois' influential article, "The Structure and Classification of Games." In that

TABLE 1   Caillois' Classification of Games

	AGON Competitions	ALEA Chance	MIMICRY Pretence	ILINI Vertigo
PAIDIA				
Noise	Races (not	Comptines	Childish	Children's swings
Agitation	regulated)	Heads or tails	imitation	Merry-go-round
Laughter	Combats			Teeter-totter
Dance	Athletics		Masks	Waltz
Hoop			Costumes	
Solitaire	Boxing	Betting		
Games	Fencing	Roulette	Theatre	Outdoor sports
of patience	Football			Skiing
Crossword	Checkers	Lotteries		Mountain
puzzles	Chess			climbing
LUDUS				

---

[12] impulsive: acting suddenly and without thinking or reflecting

article, Caillois adopts a modified version of Huizinga's definition of play and then goes on to treat play and games as synonymous terms. As a consequence, games staged for mass entertainment by paid professionals, being far more like work than play, would not be covered by Caillois' classification. His classification of games can also be criticized for being too broad. While kite flying, waltzing, and riding merry-go-rounds can easily be subsumed[13] under the heading play, it would be straining a bit to call them games.

10   If Caillois' work is viewed as a classification of play only, the above-mentioned difficulties immediately disappear. In fact, when viewed in this light, Caillois' classification makes significant contributions to the understanding of the play phenomenon. One of Caillois' key contributions is his classification of play forms by the motives of participants. Some types of play are primarily competitive; others depend on chance or fate. Still others are appealing because they give one a chance to indulge in pretense[14] or to achieve a feeling of vertigo[15]. Caillois calls these motives agon, alea, mimicry, and ilini respectively. Caillois' other major contribution is his recognition that play can be relatively spontaneous and unstructured (paidia) or highly regulated and organized (ludus). This classification of play by motive and degree of normative regulation is a significant addition to, and refinement of, Huizinga's formulations.

11   The problem still remains, however, of finding an adequate definition for the term game. John Loy is somewhat more precise in distinguishing between games and play than is Caillois. According to Loy, a game is "any form of playful competition whose outcome is determined by physical skill, strategy or chance employed singly or in combination." This goes beyond Caillois' rather loose usage of the term game by adding the idea of competition. For Loy, games always involve a struggle to win. Competition may be with individuals, teams, animate and inanimate objects, or with ideal standards. When defined in this way, playful activities like flying kites, riding teeter-totters or dressing up in costumes, would not be treated as games unless these activities were somehow to become competitive.

12   Loy's definition, while helping to separate the concepts of play and game, still fails to deal adequately with professional games. This is because by defining a game as

---

[13] subsume: to include as a part of a larger group
[14] pretense: a way of behaving that is meant to deceive people
[15] vertigo: a dizzy or spinning feeling

a "playful" competition, he ends up making it a subcategory of play. It is this writer's contention that to define professional sport in terms of play is to distort its most essential features. Drawing on the discussion of work and play presented at the outset of this paper, it is obvious that the games of professionals fall far toward the work end of the work-play continuum. The professional ballplayer, even when he enjoys his work, cannot escape the fact that his sport participation is a task, to which he is obliged to submit. If he misses a game or a practice session he may be fined or in some other way sanctioned. This obviously violates the freedom so critical to play.

13   It is also clear, contrary to what Loy has argued, that professional games are as productive and utilitarian[16] in motive as any other work activity. The professional ballplayer is well aware that he is laboring to make a living and the pressures of the workaday world are constantly intruding into his games. He can hardly ignore the fact that a series of "blown" plays, bad games, or serious injuries can put an end to his career and threaten the well-being of himself or his family. The product he produces is entertainment and the payment he receives is financial security. Upon hearing the final gun that ends his game, the professional athlete is as likely to express feelings of relief, as is any other worker when a whistle ends his working day. Professional games then, inasmuch as they (1) involve activity that participants are obliged to perform (2) are oriented to the pragmatic concerns of ordinary life, and (3) are pursued for profit or material gain, share almost nothing in common with play.

14   What is necessary to improve Loy's definition of a game, therefore, is the addition of the idea that games can be both play and work. The following definition, expanding Loy's somewhat, allows the introduction of this idea: A game is any form of competition, staged primarily for the enjoyment of either participants or spectators, whose outcome is determined by physical skill, strategy, or chance employed singly or in combination. Such a definition allows for the inclusion of games produced by professionals. When the entertainment needs of spectators are given highest priority, games tend to become work. When the sheer joy of participation is emphasized, the play element reigns supreme.

Sport, Play and Work

15   Having discussed the concepts of play, work, and games, it remains to examine their relationship to sport. Probably the best way to distinguish between a game and a sport is to treat a game as a unique event and a sport as a pattern. Loy, following this

---

[16] utilitarian: useful and practical

approach, defines sport as "an institutionalized game demanding a demonstration of physical prowess." What this means is that the sport of American football, for instance, consists of the formalized norms, which have crystallized[17] over the past 100 years to regulate the behavior of modern-day football players. Sport then, is a more or less stable pattern of culture and social structure. It has a history and will be passed on into the future. A game, on the other hand, is a concrete event. That is, it is an actual acting out or occurrence of a sport.

16   Although satisfactory in most respects, Loy's definition is in need of some refinement. First, it is obvious that the inadequacies of his definition of the term "game," discussed above, will carry over into his definition of sport. The result is that professional sport is misrepresented as play. The revised definition of games this writer presented above serves to eliminate this problem. Another refinement of Loy's conception of sport would be to distinguish among institutionalized games which demand varying degrees of physical prowess. For instance, it might be useful to separate sports like pool, bowling, or archery from ice hockey, football, and cross-country ski racing. The former, while demanding high levels of physical skill, do not demand total physical involvement to the point of bodily exhaustion. It is only the participants in the latter activities, because of the sheer physical endurance demanded, that should be referred to as athletes. More will be said on this later.

17   In summary, it can be said that the basic problem with definitional efforts discussed so far is that they tend to treat all sport as play and are thereby inadequate for dealing with professional sport.

Sport and Play as Opposites

18   Having dealt with the problem of confounding[18] sport with play, it is now necessary to discuss an error in the opposite direction. That is, some writers argue that sport has nothing whatsoever in common with play. This argument receives its clearest expression in the work of Harry Edwards.

According to Edwards, as one moves from play to sport the following occurs:

1. Activity becomes less subject to individual prerogative, with spontaneity severely diminished.

2. Separation from the rigors and pressures of daily life becomes less prevalent.

---

[17] crystallize: to become definite and permanent in form
[18] confound: confuse, treat different ideas as if they were the same

3. The relevance of the outcome of the activity and the individual's role in it extends to groups and collectivities that do not participate directly in the act.

4. Goals become diverse, complex, and more related to values emanating from outside of the context of the activity.

5. Formal rules and structural role and position relationships and responsibilities within the activity assume predominance.

6. Individual liability and responsibility for the quality and character of his behavior during the course of the activity is heightened.

7. The activity consumes a greater proportion of the individual's time and attention due to the need for preparation and the degree of seriousness involved in the act.

8. The emphasis upon physical and mental extension beyond the limits of refreshment or interest in the act assumes increasing dominance.

19   It is this writer's contention that of the eight criteria Edwards uses to distinguish play from sport, the first four actually highlight quite effectively the key difference between play and professional sport. What Edwards is saying is that sport, like work, imposes severe limitations on an individual's freedom, is immersed in the pressures and concerns of ordinary life, and is always pursued for rewards which lie outside of the sphere of play itself. It is obvious that for Edwards, sport and professional sport are virtually synonymous terms and have little, if anything, in common with play. The last four criteria, it can be argued, are of no value whatever for distinguishing between the concepts play and sport because they focus on qualities that vary considerably within play itself. The major problem with Edwards' definitional effort, however, is that it makes playful sport logically impossible.

20   In Edwards' scheme, racketball between friends, if entered freely, kept separate from the pressures of the workaday world, and pursued for no material gain or profit cannot constitute a sport. This is true regardless of the fact that the rules of racketball are rigidly codified[19] and institutionalized, its participants often push themselves unmercifully, and players get tremendous self satisfaction from improving the quality of their games. Likewise, mountain climbing pursued voluntarily and solely for the intrinsic rewards one gains from a competitive struggle against nature, would not be a sport by Edwards' definition. The climber may train on his own to develop his

---

[19] codified: formally stated, often in writing

climbing skills, he may ultimately push himself to the limits of human endurance and expose himself to conditions few would endure for any price. Yet, because he enters this activity freely, has no desire for rewards other than those derived from climbing itself, and accomplishes his end without being driven by authoritarian coaches and screaming hoards of spectators, this climber cannot, according to Edwards, call his efforts sport.

21   It would appear that Edwards, like so many people in the world of sport, assumes that physical competition is only taken seriously when pursued by skilled professionals in rationalized and commercialized settings. The assumption is that those who play at their games are not concerned with the quality and outcome of their performances. Admittedly, play may at times be little more than "fun and games." However, playful competition can also be undertaken with an intensity that is unsurpassed[20] in even the most highly organized professional contests. To assume that human beings will strive[21] for bodily excellence only when under compulsion[22], or when seeking financial gain is to underestimate the potential of playful or truly amateur sport.

An Attempt at Synthesis

22   At this point, an attempt to construct a typology[23] of sport utilizing elements from each of the formulations criticized above is in order. Along with Edwards, I feel that play and sport must at times be treated as polar opposites, but only when play

TABLE 2   A Typology of Sport

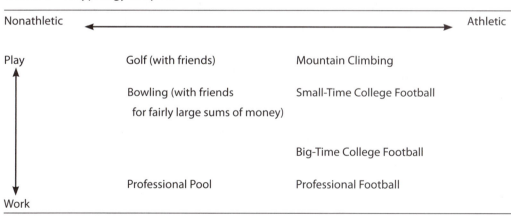

Nonathletic		Athletic
Play		
	Golf (with friends)	Mountain Climbing
	Bowling (with friends for fairly large sums of money)	Small-Time College Football
		Big-Time College Football
	Professional Pool	Professional Football
Work		

---

[20] unsurpassed: not exceeded
[21] strive: to make a serious effort to achieve something
[22] under compulsion: the act of being forced to do something, compelled
[23] typology: a system of classification

is contrasted with professional sport. Edwards errs by ignoring those forms of sport activity that should properly be regarded as play. Like Loy and Caillois, I would argue that some forms of sport can best be defined as a subcategory of play. The weakness of their formulations, however, is that they tend to misrepresent sport activity that should properly be regarded as work. To eliminate some of these shortcomings, a typology of sport is needed that is broad enough to treat sport as both work and play.

23   Another distinction which should be made within sport itself is between athletic and nonathletic sport. All sport, by definition, is dependent on physical prowess. However, as Weiss, Edwards, and others have argued, only if one makes a concerted physical effort, involving exertion to the limits of fatigue and endurance, can one be an athlete participating in a game. By dividing the realm of sport along a dimension of nonathletic and athletic sport, the following typology emerges.

24   In the above typology, sport is defined as an institutionalized game, dependent on physical prowess. A game is defined as any form of competition, staged for the enjoyment of either participants or spectators whose outcome is determined by physical skill, strategy, or chance employed singly or in combination. Play and work represent ideal types, i.e., mental constructs composed of the most characteristic or essential elements of each phenomenon. All game occurrences of sport fall along a continuum from play to work. It should also be noted that some types of sport fall somewhere between the athletic and nonathletic. Golf, shuffleboard, bowling, and curling are examples which come to mind. Thus, the area between athletic and nonathletic sport must also be viewed as a continuum linking two ideal types.

25   The main advantage of the typology of sport developed in this paper is that it builds on earlier formulations but at the same time makes explicit the fact that sport can occur as both work and play.

REFERENCES

Caillois, R. (1969). The structure and classification of games. In J. Loy & G. Kenyon (Eds.), *Sport, culture and society*. (pp. 44–45). New York: Macmillan.

Edwards, H. (1973). *Sociology of sport*. (pp. 43–61). Homewood, IL: Dorsey.

Huizinga, J. (1959). *Homo ludens*. Boston: Beacon Press, pp. 1–27.

Loy, J. W. (1969). The nature of sport. In J. Loy & G. Kenyon (Eds.), *Sport, culture and society*. (pp. 56–71). London: Macmillan.

Getting at the Matter

In this reading, Sack builds on the work of other scholars in order to critically examine the idea of sport and its relationship to several other related ideas: play, game, *and* work. *Working either independently or with a small group, complete these tasks.*

1. Use the chart to summarize Sack's analysis. Check the concepts that each scholar has discussed, and indicate the strengths and weaknesses of their ideas according to Sack.

Huizinga ☐ Game ☐ Play ☐ Sport ☐ Work	Strengths: Weaknesses:
Caillois ☐ Game ☐ Play ☐ Sport ☐ Work	Strengths: Weaknesses:
Loy ☐ Game ☐ Play ☐ Sport ☐ Work	Strengths: Weaknesses:
Edwards ☐ Game ☐ Play ☐ Sport ☐ Work	Strengths: Weaknesses:

2. In your own words, explain Sack's typology of sport as illustrated in Table 2, p. 143.

Academic Vocabulary Focus

Fifteen passages taken from the reading "Sport: Play or Work?" or related to it follow. Each passage highlights a word from the AWL. Read each passage and try to come up with a synonym or phrase that means about the same thing as the highlighted word. If you have any difficulties, select a synonym for the highlighted word from the bulleted list.

- create
- require
- show
- happen
- direct toward

- precisely stated
- current
- continue
- go against
- control

- stop
- encourage
- receive
- improve upon
- agree to

1. Many **contemporary** discussions of the play concept find their starting point in Johan Huizinga's classic work *Homo Ludens* in which Huizinga emphasizes the most important features of play, particularly its free, voluntary nature.

2. In *The Structure and Classification of Games,* Roger Caillois **refines** Huizinga's ideas, but in the process he makes the mistake of treating the concepts of play and game as synonymous.

3. John Loy's analysis **reveals** the limitations in Callois' analysis and distinguishes more clearly the differences between the concepts of play and game.

4. Allen Sack, in the article *Sport: Play or Work?* synthesizes the ideas of Huizinga, Callois, Loy, and Edwards and **formulates** a typology of sport that further clarifies the relationships between concepts like play, game, and sport.

5. Although everyone has an intuitive sense of the meaning of sport, this essay tries to make these intuitions **explicit.**

6. According to Huizinga, play can be **suspended** at any time; it is never an obligation.

7. Professional sport, like work, **imposes** severe limitations on an individual's freedom.

8. Strictly speaking, professional baseball is not play. The professional ballplayer, even when he enjoys his work, cannot escape the fact that his sport participation is a task to which he is obliged to **submit.**

Thinking Beyond the Content

9. If a professional player misses a game or a practice session he may be fined or in some other way sanctioned. This obviously **violates** the freedom so critical to play.

10. Generally speaking, the more an activity is a task or obligation **oriented** to the pragmatic concerns of making a living and pursued for profit or material interest, the more it approximates work.

11. Coaches and sports organizations often **promote** sports for children and youth by insisting that they build character in the young athlete.

12. The NCAA (National Collegiate Athletic Association) is an organization that **regulates** inter-collegiate sports.

13. After an interruption caused by a protest by an angry coach, for which the coach was penalized, the basketball game **proceeded** smoothly.

14. The penalty **occurred** during the first half of the game.

15. The non-competitive gymnast **derives** satisfaction purely from the process of gradual improvement and mastery of his or her own body.

For Discussion

Respond to the questions with a partner or small group.

1. Apply Sack's insights to one or more of the opening scenarios from Blanchard's "The Meaning of Sport." Use Sack's criteria for differentiating the terms *game, play, sport* and *work*. Analyze the scenario as completely as you can.

2. Can you find any problem(s) with the typology of sport that Sack has described? What modifications in Sack's depiction can you suggest to address the problem(s)?

Reading 2

Pre-Reading

Respond to the prompts in a short essay, or discuss them with a partner or small group.

1. Name as many sports as you can that are popular in your country.

2. Are you familiar with any strange or unusual sports, ancient or modern? If so describe them for your partner or group mates.

Thinking Beyond the Content

READING 2: The Meaning of Sport—A Cultural Approach

Kendall Blanchard

From Blanchard, K. (1995). The anthropology of sport. *Westport, CT: Bergin & Garvey, pp. 27–60.*

In "The Meaning of Sport," anthropologist Kendall Blanchard acknowledges that sport sociologists have had some success developing a theory of sport that includes an acceptable definition of sport. However, in this article Blanchard focuses on the difficulties of trying to apply these definitions across cultures and even to popular activities within a culture. He shows that when we move further away from conventional sports like football or basketball, or when we observe the activities of unfamiliar cultures, our concepts may break down.

Blanchard's article is an entertaining introduction to the problem of studying sport from an anthropological point of view, providing the reader with a number of interesting puzzles. Since the article was written in 1995, some of the examples may be out of date, but the points they are intended to illustrate are no less relevant today than they were in 1995.

An effective way to read this article is to pause at those points in the article where Blanchard poses challenging questions and try to answer these questions before continuing.

1   Consider the following activities and situations:

   1. A demolition derby[24] on a small-town, dirt track speedway in southeastern Georgia on a hot, muggy[25] August night.

   2. Eddie Murray[26] walks onto the football field with six seconds left to play, kicks a forty-five yard field goal, wins the game for the Dallas Cowboys[27] and walks back to the bench.

   3. A group of dusty farmers, small-time business men, and full-time ne'er-do-wells[28] are crowded into an old barn in backwoods Tennessee watching two specially trained roosters[29] fight to the death.

   4. A teenager hangs over a Street-Fighter II machine[30] in a suburban Philadelphia convenience store, literally working up a sweat in the attempt to better his own record score.

   5. A Norwegian figure skater does a complicated routine to Ravel's "Bolero" and scores a 9.6 in an international figure skating championship.

   6. A high school couple in Chico, California dances a highly stylized version of the "jitterbug" and wins a 1950s-style dance contest.

2   Which of these activities would you describe as sport? Can you isolate the rationale that you used in making those decisions? If you are like most, you will find yourself faced with indecision on both counts. Sport is not always easy to recognize. It is sometimes said of "play" that, although it is difficult to define, one knows it when one sees it. Sport is more specialized than play, and may not afford the same convenience.

3   Recognizing sport is even more difficult when one is put into a cultural setting other than his or her own. Consider the "song duel"[31] of the Eskimos, or, as they are more appropriately referred to today, the Inuit[32].

---

[24] demolition derby: a contest in which drivers crash old cars into one another trying to disable the opponents' cars. The winner is the last car running.

[25] muggy: humid

[26] Eddie Murray: a former field goal kicker for the Dallas Cowboys, an American football team, during the 1993 and 1999 seasons.

[27] Dallas Cowboys: an American professional football team located in Dallas, Texas

[28] ne'er-do-well: a worthless person who never does anything useful or productive

[29] rooster: adult male chicken

[30] Street Fighter II machine: a kind of video game

[31] duel: formal combat between two individuals that is usually observed by witnesses

[32] Inuit: Native American people that lived in the far north in North America and in Greenland

Thinking Beyond the Content

4 Among many Inuit groups in the traditional North American Arctic, an institution called the "song duel" is frequently used to adjudicate[33] criminal offenses or manage potentially dangerous disputes. For example, if a man steals another man's wife, the bereaved husband might challenge the offender to a song duel. If the latter is amenable[34], a time and place is arranged and the two meet in head-to-head competition. The rest of the community turns out in force; the spectators will determine a winner, so they are vital to the song duel. Besides, what else is there to do on a long, frigid night in the snow-covered Arctic?

5 The "song duel" is a battle of words and wit[35]. Combatants mimic[36], parody[37], and shout abusive, though often creative, insults at each other. Each puts on a show. The audience is entertained. They laugh with each nasty, cutely phrased accusation and applaud the well-designed, choreographed antics[38] of the duelers. Anderson (1974/75:76–77) has recorded the words of a famous song duel that took place among the Kobuk River Eskimo in the late nineteenth century as these are recounted in community oral history. The exchange begins with the song of Akausraurak:

> Immok, I wish, I want to use your legs.
> I would like to walk around using them.
> Immok, I wish I could borrow your funny legs,
> The ones you used to go see your brother's wife, Immok.

Immok sings in response:

> Akausraurak likes to use my legs.
> Real good, respected man shouldn't use my legs because he might become
>   an idiot.
> My legs are not to go tell my relatives to go away from me,
> My legs are simply good for crossing the creeks without having to use a boat.

6 The object of the duel from the participants' standpoint[39] is to gain the sympathy and support of the audience. The singer who is successful in working the audience so that it laughs with him and at his opponent is the winner of the competition. So every effort is made to court the spectators, using both word and dance, with the movement designed

---

[33] adjudicate: to settle a legal dispute
[34] amenable: willing
[35] wit: ability to use words in a clever or humorous way
[36] mimic: imitate
[37] parody: copy the style of someone or something in a humorous way
[38] antic: playful, funny action intended to get attention
[39] standpoint: perspective, point of view

to amplify[40] the message of the song as well as to flaunt[41] one's physical prowess[42]. Eventually, the sympathies of the crowd become clear; its language suggests that it has decided in favor of one of the two combatants. The reaction eventually makes clear the victory of one and the defeat of the other.

7   The untrained outsider not familiar with the song duel when asked to characterize the institution might respond in one of several ways. Like the blind man attempting to describe the elephant, his response is affected by the particular dimension of the song duel that he perceives. One observer might be impressed by the rhythm of the songs, the occasional mention of supernatural figures, and the emotional involvement of the spectators, and call the song duel a "religious ritual." Another might notice the feasting that sometimes takes place in this context and suggest that the song duel is a playful part of a community picnic. An astute student of human behavior might notice the gift giving and interpret the event as an informal market in which reciprocity and the exchange of goods is facilitated. Yet another observer might delve[43] into the events leading up to the song duel and explore the consequences of the event. Such confrontations can have serious repercussions[44]; there have been situations in which defeat has brought with it such chagrin[45] that the losers have committed suicide. Having taken all this into consideration, this latter observer might call the "song duel" a "primitive court" system in which the community acts as jury to determine what is just in a confrontation between litigants[46]. Finally, one observer, the one with the running shoes who plays squash and has season tickets to the Knicks[47], home games, might remark, "By golly, that's sport, if I ever saw it." And, he could make a good case for his observation. The song duel is playful and competitive, has physical dimensions, involves the eventual declaration of a winner and loser, and has been described by others as sporting. Hoebel (1954:99), for example, has remarked that "as the court-room joust[48] may become a sporting game between attorneys-at-law, so the juridical song contest is above all things a contest in which pleasurable delight is richly served, so richly that the dispute-settlement function is nearly forgotten."

8   So, which observer is correct? In one sense, all are right; in another, none. This is the dilemma of behavior definition and classification, a dilemma to which anthropologists are extremely sensitive and one that necessitates a discussion about the concept "sport" and its definition.

---

[40] amplify: to expand, enlarge, and provide more detail
[41] flaunt: display in an obvious, immodest way
[42] prowess: combination of strength, skill, and courage
[43] delve: carefully examine, research
[44] repercussions: consequences, especially not anticipated
[45] chagrin: bad feeling brought about by humiliation or failure
[46] litigant: someone involved in a lawsuit
[47] Knicks: the New York Knickerbockers, a professional basketball team
[48] joust: one-on-one combat or competition

Thinking Beyond the Content

9 For the most part, key terms such as "play," "game," "leisure," and "recreation," as well as "sport," are yet to be assigned meanings that are generally agreed upon by anthropologists, or for that matter, by any general group of social scientists. Anthropologist-physical educator Allan Tindall (1976:3) has put this problem into perspective for those dealing with sport and recreation on an international level. Noting that such terms are "loaded with European bias," he suggests that:

> it is highly unlikely that the terms "sport" or physical education occur in direct parallel in languages of a non-European origin. In the literature with which I am familiar "sport" has no definitive meaning or referent. Many disparate types of activities are labeled "sport." Professional and amateur athletic competition as well as hunting and fishing activities are all labeled sport. As I look across the usages of the term I find neither a consistent use of the word with reference to patterns of human movement or goal orientations (Tindall, 1976:3).

10 Most of the early literature on sport behavior ignores the conceptual problem and simply assumes that readers know what is meant by terms like "play" or "leisure." For example, in his "Ethnologie des Sports" (1925), Weule discusses at length the evolution of sport and its various expressions among historic primitive peoples, but at no time does he define the term "sport." More recently, similar omissions are obvious in works like Menke's (1947) *Encyclopedia of Sports* and Gipe's (1978) *The Great American Sports Book*. In the Human Relations Area Files (HRAF) a wide range of activities are grouped in section 526, "athletic sports," without any further definitional treatment. Some comparative studies, such as Sipe's (1973) "War, Sports and Aggression," have been based on the file materials, and some researchers have overlooked[49] conceptual matters, assuming that the HRAF classification was self-explanatory and of legitimate transcultural application.

11 To the sport sociologists' credit, much of their theoretical writing in recent years has focused on the problem of definition. Important publications on the subject include Caillois's (1969) "The Structure and Classification of Games," Edwards' (1973) *Sociology of Sport,* Kenyon's (1969) "A Conceptual Model for Characterizing Physical Activity," Loy's (1969) "The Nature of Sport," Nixon's (1990) "Rethinking Socialization and Sport," Sack's (1977b) "Sport: Play or Work?," and Yiannakis' (1989) "Toward an Applied Sociology of Sport: The Next Generation." However, while these works have led to some clarification, many definitional difficulties remain, especially when one approaches the issue from an anthropological perspective.

---

[49] overlook: miss, fail to see

12 One of the conceptual problems that the anthropology of sport must contend with is the fact that some of its key terms are without equivalents in many languages. Some groups do not make a clear distinction between work and play, different forms of games, or sport and ritual. Also, physically combative sports are simply nonexistent in some societies (Sipes, 1973:69). In many cases, extenuating circumstances (e.g., climate, work schedules) may obviously prohibit such sport activities, so simple structural explanations, those taking only the rules and equipment into account, are often not sufficient to explain the presence or absence of the phenomenon, thus further complicating the analysis.

REFERENCES

Anderson, W. W. (1974/1975). Song duel of the Kobuk River Eskimo. *Folk, 16*(17), 73–81.

Caillois, R. (1969). The structure and classification of games. In J. Loy & G. Kenyon (Eds.), *Sport, culture and society.* (pp. 44–45). New York: Macmillan.

Edwards, H. (1973). *Sociology of sport.* Homewood, IL: Dorsey Press.

Gipe, G. (1978). *The great American sports book.* Garden City, NY: Doubleday.

Hoebel, E. A. (1954/1972). *The law of primitive man.* New York: Atheneum.

Kenyon, G. (1969). A conceptual model for characterizing physical activity. In J. Loy & G. Kenyon (Eds.), *Sport, culture and society* (pp. 71–81).New York: Macmillan.

Loy, J. W. (1969). The nature of sport. In J. Loy & G. Kenyon (Eds.), *Sport, culture and society.* (pp. 56–71).
New York: Macmillan.

Menke, Frank G. (1947/1960). *The new encyclopedia of sports.* New York: A. S. Barnes.

Nixon, Howard L. (1990). Rethinking socialization and sport. *Journal of Sport and Social Issues, 14*(1), 33–47.

Sack, A. L. (1977). Sport: Play or work? In P. Stevens, Jr. (Ed.), *Studies in the anthropology of play.* (pp. 186-195).West Point, NY: Leisure Press.

Sipes, Richard. (1973). War, sports, and aggression: An empirical test of two rival theories. *American Anthropologist, 75*(1),64–86.

Tindall, B. Allan. (1976 April). *Questions about physical education, skill, and lifetime leisure sports participation.* Position paper presented to UNESCO on behalf of the Association for the Anthropological Study of Play. First International Conference of Ministers and Senior Officials Responsible for Physical Education and Sport for Youth.

von Weule, K. (1925). Ethnologie des sportes. In G. A. E. Boegeng (Ed.), *Geschichte des sportes aller Volker und Zeiten,* Leipzig.

Yiannakis, A. (1989). Toward an applied sociology of sport: The next generation. *Sociology of Sport Journal, 6*(1), 1–16.

Getting at the Matter

Answer the questions in writing. Then discuss your responses with one or more partners.

1. What is the main point that the author makes in this excerpt?

2. Why does the author describe the song duel of the Inuit in such detail? Do you consider the song duel to be an example of sport? Why or why not?

3. In what ways does the song duel resemble a spectator sport? In what ways is it different from spectator sports that you are familiar with?

4. Describe the difficulties the anthropologist faces in developing a cross-cultural understanding of sport.

Critical Focus Review

One of the central purposes of this book has been to point out the critical role that citations and references play in the academic text. Like many of the readings in this book, Reading 2 contains a great number of citations. Reread "The Meaning of Sport," and pay close attention to the in-text citations and references. Then answer these questions.

1. Which paragraphs contain the greatest number of citations?

2. In general, the citations seem to fall into two major groups. What is the main difference between the two groups? Does the author seem to approve of one group of sources more than the other, or does he see them all as equally valuable? Explain.

3. If you were going to do further research on the issues raised in this reading, which of the listed references would you be most interested in reading? Identify at least three references, and explain why you would choose these rather than other ones on the reference list.

4. If you have access to an academic library, see whether you can find any of the references cited in "The Meaning of Sport." Read (or if the source is very long, skim) the article, and write or give a brief oral summary of the source.

5. Using an academic library database, see whether you can find a source more recent than the current reading that addresses the problem of defining sport. Report orally or in writing on what you discover.

Academic Vocabulary Focus

In the left-hand list are 15 words from the AWL that are used in Reading 2. Use the paragraph numbers (in parentheses) to locate the words (or related forms) in the reading. Match these words with their corresponding definitions or synonyms in the right-hand column of the chart. Use a dictionary only if necessary.

Vocabulary

_____ 1. *clarification* (Par. 11)

_____ 2. *consistent* (Par. 9)

_____ 3. *context* (Par. 7)

_____ 4. *definitive* (Par. 9)

_____ 5. *eventual(ly)* (Par. 6, 7)

_____ 6. *facilitate* (Par. 7)

_____ 7. *ignore* (Par. 10)

_____ 8. *institution* (Par. 4, 7)

_____ 9. *interpret* (Par. 7)

_____ 10. *isolate* (Par. 2)

_____ 11. *label* (Par. 9)

_____ 12. *obvious(ly)* (Par. 10, 12)

_____ 13. *perspective* (Par. 9, 11)

_____ 14. *structure* (Par. 11, 12)

_____ 15. *version* (Par. 1)

Definition/Synonym

a. separate

b. customary practice or way of doing something

c. help, make possible

d. not notice, not pay attention to

e. explanation that makes something clear and understandable

f. easy to notice or understand

g. to describe or to give a name to

h. the same, not in conflict

i. alternate form or variety

j. point of view, way of looking at things

k. arrangement or relationship between parts

l. background, circumstance, environment

m. explain, understand

n. best, most complete, most widely agreed upon

o. at a later time

For Discussion

Discuss these questions in a small group. Then share your opinions with the class.

1. What is physical education? Is it synonymous with sport? Does physical education play any role in the school curriculum in your country? If so, what ideas and activities constitute physical education?

2. In Paragraph 9, Blanchard notes that in addition to the term *sport*, the terms *play, game, leisure,* and *recreation* have no agreed upon definitions. How would you define each of these terms? Compare and contrast the meanings and uses of various pairs of terms. For instance, what is the relationship between the terms *sport* and *game*? Is every sport a game? Is every game a sport? Use examples whenever possible to explain your ideas. (You may need to use sources to help you clarify how these terms are used in English. You might even want to consider interviewing a native speaker.)

Reading 3

Pre-Reading

Before reading the selection, discuss the questions with a partner or small group.

1. Do you currently participate, or have you ever participated, regularly in some sport? If so, what did you like about participating?

2. Do you like to watch sports? Why or why not?

3. Which statement best expresses your opinion?
   _____ a. I prefer to play sports.
   _____ b. I prefer to watch sports.
   _____ c. I am not particularly interested in either playing or watching sports

4. Are spectator sports popular in your country? What reasons can you give for their popularity (or unpopularity)?

Thinking Beyond the Content

READING 3: Why Competition Excites Us

Ellis Cashmore

From Cashmore, E. (2005). Making sense of sports (4th ed.). *New York: Routledge. pp. 1–11.*

The first two readings in the unit have dealt with the problem of trying to define sport, first from a sociological point of view, then from an anthropological point of view. With this final reading, we will set the problem of definition aside and ask a psychological question. Why do so many people seem to be drawn to competitive sports either as players or as spectators? Ellis Cashmore, professor of Culture, Media and Sport in the School of Health at Staffordshire University in England, addresses this question in "Why Competition Excites Us." Cashmore's essay is not a survey of all possible answers to the question, but he does elaborate on a popular and often repeated explanation: Sport satisfies primitive human instincts that cannot be satisfied in a modern world so different from the world in which human beings evolved.

As a critical reader, you may want to set aside any temptation you may have to immediately agree with this explanation. You may want to try to think beyond the text and try to propose some alternative explanations.

Because Life's Too Predictable

1   "The why of a fan" is the title of an article published in the *North American Review* way back in 1929 in which A. A. Brill argued that "life organized too well becomes monotonous[50]; too much peace and security breed boredom; and old instincts, bred into the very cells of the body . . . still move the masses of normal men" (1929: 431). (Year of publication followed by a colon and page numbers quoted appear in parentheses.)

2   Brill wrote in terms of the "restrictions of modern life" depriving people of their "activity and scope, the triumphs[51] and *réclame*" which were achievable through physical prowess[52] under "more primitive conditions" (*réclame* means renown or notoriety—what we'd now regard as celebrity). In explaining the fans' attraction to sport, Brill exposed what he took to be a dark truth about human nature; he described the human being as "an animal formed for battle and conquest, for blows and strokes and swiftness, for triumph and applause" (1929: 434).

3   As the civilizing process and rise of governing states removed the necessity for physical struggle and modernity[53] brought with it order, stability and security, so the nasty[54] and brutish[55] qualities were made redundant[56]—but not irrelevant. They were of great use in sport. The sports that began to take shape in the middle of the nineteenth century required physical prowess. Of course, not everyone could excel in physical activities; but the ones who couldn't were able to identify with those who could.

4   In Brill's view, this enabled them to recover something of their natural state; they could "achieve exaltation[57], vicarious[58] but real" and be "a better individual, better citizen." Sports, or at least its precursors, actually contributed to building a better citizenry for the modern nation state.

5   Improbable as Brill's argument might have been as a total theory of sport, it offered a timeless insight about the drabness[59] and formality ushered in by modernity, which is often thought to have begun in the Enlightenment of the eighteenth century and had effects across all facets of society. One of the effects of the modern effort to bring shape and coherence to human affairs was that life became more directed, more patterned, and more predictable.

---

[50] monotonous: unchanging, boring

[51] triumph: joy in victory or success

[52] prowess: combination of strength, skill, and courage

[53] modernity: modern times

[54] nasty: unpleasant, disgusting

[55] brutish: crude, animal like

[56] redundant: extra, more than what is necessary

[57] exaltation: intense sense of well-being

[58] vicarious: experienced as a result of watching, listening to, or reading about the activities of other people, rather than by doing the activities yourself

[59] drabness: lacking in color, dull, monotonous, boring

Thinking Beyond the Content

6   The German social theorist Max Weber used the term *calculability* to capture the ethos[60] of modern bureaucracy; he meant that the workings of the complex organizations that proliferated[61] all around him (he was writing around 1904–20) strained towards regulation. The rules and procedures were designed to minimize the intrusion of the personal emotions or whims[62] of those who administered its policies. As a result, the performance of a bureaucracy was highly predictable.

7   Once the applicable regulations and procedures are known, it's possible to calculate exactly how a bureaucracy is going to deal with a matter and predict the likelihood of a certain type of outcome. So bureaucracies stabilize a society, order its policies, regulate its citizens, and make it reliably predictable. All this makes for a rational and smooth-running society. It also affects the mentality[63] of people who live in such a society.

8   Calculability is an organizing principle in all contemporary societies, apart from those in the throes[64] of upheaval. Spontaneity[65] and randomness may be pleasant diversions[66] but, in large doses[67], they can prove disruptive[68] and threaten the citizenry's sense of security. Still, there is a residual attraction in the unplanned, surprise happening; everyone knows the pleasant sensation of an unexpected gift or a turn of events that are completely unexpected. On an occasional basis, surprises are fine; were they to invade our working, or public lives, they would lead to disruption and, possibly, disorientation.

9   In the main, we try to confine the fascination for the unpredictable to our private lives. Office workers can approach their daily tasks with a strangulating[69] regard to rationality and precision. Once out of the office, they might retreat to the tumult[70] of home where chaos, clutter, and utter confusion reigns. One set of rules for the office, but another for home.

10   The separation of life into public and private spheres is itself a product of the modern age. It has the advantage of allowing the individual to compensate in one sphere for the tensions and frustrations that build up in the other. How many of us have quietly boiled in rage during a lecture or at work? We might keep a lid on[71] it, but explode once we're in a different context. Most of us experience bureaucracies, if only indirectly, and, equally, most of us have been irritated or angered by them; but we typically don't scream or assault people. Instead, we find outlets for these emotions elsewhere—like in sports.

---

[60] ethos: the way of thinking and behaving typical of a group during a particular time in history
[61] proliferate: increase greatly in number
[62] whim: sudden unexpected idea
[63] mentality: way of thinking, perspective
[64] throes: difficult and painful struggles
[65] spontaneity: sudden impulsive, unplanned action
[66] diversion: something done to entertain or amuse
[67] dose: measured portion or amount
[68] disruptive: causing a break or interruption from the normal order
[69] strangulating: constrictive, causing the flow of a substance to stop
[70] tumult: disorder, noise, and confusion
[71] keep a lid on: control

11   Kicking or throwing balls, riding horses in a circle, or inflicting pointless damage on others might look like irrational pursuits. But that's precisely the point; whether watched or performed, they guide the participant clear of the formal limits of bureaucracies and into areas where the outcomes of situations are wholly unpredictable—the opposite of bureaucracies.

12   For all of the layer-on-layer of organization that sports have acquired, especially in recent years, the actual sporting activity has retained one special nucleus: *indeterminacy*. You can never predict the result with unerring success. That is, unless the result is fixed; but then it ceases to be a genuine sport and becomes a fake or just plain theater. The indeterminate qualities of sports make them constant challenges to the bureaucratic spirit of predictability. The result of a competition can never be determined in advance, even when the odds overwhelmingly favor one party over another. Athletic competition is an area where fairytale endings occasionally do come true. Every underdog[72] has a shot at winning.

. . .And Too Civil

13   The British writer Howard Jacobson has offered a short but provocative account of our fascination with sports. Like Brill, he relies on a primitive model of the human being as engaged in a sort of struggle against the civilizing influences of contemporary life. Sport is an outlet for our lust for killing, "the aestheticization of the will to murder," as Jacobson calls it in his article. "We need bad behaviour in sport it's the way to win" (in *The Independent,* June 6, 1998).

14   Jacobson appeals to Darwin's theory of natural selection; he believes that life is itself a form of competition, though human society cannot function on a win-at-all-cost principle. So we've devised manners, customs, protocols, the patterns of restraint by which we live in civil society. "Which is why we have invented sport," writes Jacobson.

15   Our primary instincts incline us toward competition in order to survive, yet civil society forces us to curb those instincts or at least channel them into "the means whereby we can obey our primary instinct to prevail while adhering to the artificial forms of civilized behaviour." Jacobson goes on, "We watch sport in the hope that we may see someone die, or failing that, humiliated. We give up our weekends to witness rage, violence, unreason . . . to be part of the unrelenting hysteria of species survival, but at a safe distance."

16   In other words, it is bloodletting by proxy; we let others—the athletes—play out our instinctual impulses. This is why we feel indifferent about some sports performers who are technically good, but "nice," yet we give our hearts to headcases[73] who seem to epitomize the rage we sometimes feel inside us.

17   On this admittedly extreme view, a pool table or a tennis court, a football field or a baseball diamond is a symbolic killing field: a refined Roman Colosseum where real

---

[72] underdog: a person considered to be the weakest and the least likely to win
[73] headcase: (slang) a crazy person, someone with a mental problem

deaths actually did occur. All fulfill the same function: providing a stage on which to mount a ritualized Darwinian survival of the fittest. We the spectators are effectively electing others to do the dirty work for us. This makes for an attractive spectacle: murder rendered aesthetically pleasing for the masses.

18   Jacobson's perspective is open to many objections, not least because it crudely reduces a complex series of activities to a basic survival impulse. Yet, it provides an intriguing starting-point for discussion: sports as symbolic expressions of an impelling force that has its sources in our survival instincts. If we didn't have sports, we might be still splitting other people's heads open.

. . .And Too Safe

19   Both perspectives covered so far consider that life has become too organized and too laden with rules for our own good. There is something primeval inside us being stifled by the containing influences of modernity. Complementing this is the view that the massive changes wrought over the past two centuries have made life not only predictable and rule-bound, but also safe.

20   Of course, there are road deaths, unconquerable diseases, homicides, fatal accidents, and other unseen malefactors lurking in society, especially since 2001. Whether life is safer or less safe as a result, not so much of the September 11 attack[74] as the response to it, remains an unanswered question. One thing is certain: the intricate security arrangements that have developed since that fateful day have been designed to safeguard life rather than expose it to more risk.

21   Even allowing for 9/11 and its aftermath, our lives are a lot more secure than they were even 40 years ago, let alone in the days of barbarism. Of course, we also create new perils, like environmental pollution and nuclear energy plant catastrophes. It seems the more we find ways of minimizing danger in some areas, the more we introduce them into others.

22   The sociologist Frank Furedi argues that, by the end of the twentieth century, societies all over the world had become preoccupied, if not obsessed, by safety. Risk avoidance became an organizing principle for much behavior. Safety was not something that people could just have; they needed to work toward getting it. So human control was extended into virtually every aspect of cultural life; nothing that was potentially controllable was left to chance.

23   The title of Furedi's book Culture of Fear describes an environment in which risks are not so much there—they are created. We started to fear things that would have been taken for granted in previous times: drinking water, the nuclear family, technology; all came to be viewed as secreting previously unknown perils. Furedi despairs at this

---

[74] September 11 attack: also referred to as 9/11, the date in 2001 when nineteen terrorists belonging to the organization known as al-Qaeda hijacked four commercial airliners; two of these subsequently crashed into the two towers of the New York World Trade Center, one into the Pentagon, and one in a field in Pennsylvania.

"worship of safety," as he calls it. The most significant discoveries and innovations have arisen out of a spirit of adventure and a disregard for perils.

24 While we avoid risks that lie outside our control, we're quite prepared to take voluntary risks. The so-called "lifestyle risks" such as smoking, drinking, and driving are examples of this. But sports present us with something quite different: manufactured risks that are actually designed in such a way as to preserve natural dangers or build in new ones. Horse racing always contains some risk for both jockey and horse, particularly in steeplechases. Lowering fences would reduce the hazard, but the governing associations have resisted doing so.

25 On the other hand, boxing, especially amateur boxing, has done its utmost to reduce the dangers that are inherent in combat sports. Yet both sports are fraught with risk and both continue to prosper. According to Furedi's thesis, it is probable that they would continue to prosper with or without safety measures. He cites the example of rock climbing which had some of its risks reduced by the introduction of improved ropes, boots, helmets, and other equipment. Furedi writes: "The fact that young people who choose to climb mountains might not want to be denied the frisson[75] of risk does not enter into the calculations of the safety-conscious professional, concerned to protect us from ourselves."

26 Author of the book *Risk,* John Adams believes we have inside us a "risk thermostat" which we can set to our own tastes, according to our particular culture, or subculture: "Some like it hot—a Hell's Angel or a Grand Prix racing driver for example; others like it cool . . . But no one wants absolute zero." We all want to restore some danger to our lives. How we do it is quite interesting; for instance, the same people who go white-water rafting or bungee-jumping will probably steer clear of a restaurant declared unsafe by state sanitary inspectors.

27 A game of chess or pool might offer no hint of danger, but skiing, surfing, Xtreme sports, and all motor and air sports certainly do. Even sitting in a crowd watching these sports carries a sense of danger. And, if the crowd happens to be at a game of soccer, the danger may be not just vicarious. The risk in some sports may be tiny; but its presence is what counts; and where it doesn't exist, we invent it.

28 Seekers for the source of our attraction to sports have found it in the ways culture has changed. Complex industrial societies and the maze of bureaucratic rules and procedures they brought stifled our natural spontaneity and made life too boring, according to Brill. Our primitive urges to do battle were suppressed by the development of civility and good manners in Jacobson's view. And for others, contemporary life has become organized in such a way as to minimize risks. Sports re-inject these missing elements back into our lives. None of us is willing to sacrifice the benefits of an orderly life in which

---

[75] frisson: excitement, fear; a thrill

Thinking Beyond the Content

we are relatively safe and can go about our business without having to wonder what tomorrow will bring. At the same time, we need activities that give vent to what some writers believe to be natural impulses.

29   It seems that humans are bored: they yearn for the uncertainty, risk, danger, life lived because of instinct and passion. Sport provides an occasion for exhibiting the excesses that are prohibited in other aspects of life.

REFERENCES

Adams, J. (1995). *Risk.* London: UCL Press.
Beck, U. (1992). *Risk society.* London: Sage.
Brill, A. A. (1929). The why of a fan. *North American Review,* p. 22.
Furedi, F. (1997). *Culture of fear.* London: Cassell.

Getting at the Matter

Choose one of the questions, and answer it in a paragraph of about six to eight sentences, or discuss the question with a partner.

1. According to the author, why are sports so popular in contemporary society? Paraphrase his argument.

2. The author seems to reject the idea that human beings engage in sport purely for the sake of sport. Instead, he seems to suggest that sport is a way of compensating for something that is missing in our ordinary lives. Explain this idea in your own words.

Academic Vocabulary Focus

In the chart that follows are 15 words from the Academic Word List (AWL) that appear in the reading "Why Competition Excites Us." Use the paragraph numbers to locate each word in the reading and write its meaning in your own words. Use a dictionary to check your work.

Word	Meaning
achieve (Par. 4)	
area (Par. 11, 12, 21)	
cease (Par. 12)	
challenge (Par. 12)	
compensate (Par. 10)	
element (Par. 28)	
outcome (Par. 7, 11)	
precision (Par. 9)	
predictable (Par. 5, 6, 7, 19)	
procedure (Par. 6, 7, 28)	
pursuit (Par. 11)	
restore (Par. 26)	
retain (Par. 12)	
security (Par. 1, 3, 8, 20)	
unpredictable (Par. 9, 11)	

Now read the two paragraphs based on the ideas from "Why Competition Excites Us," and fill in each blank with an appropriate word from these choices. For grammatical accuracy, you will need to change the grammatical form of some words (i.e., include plural and third-person -s markers where appropriate). Item number 3 has been completed for you as an example.

achieve	pursue	challenge	compensate	precise
retain	unpredictable	outcome	security	restore
area	procedure	predictable	element	cease

According to some sport theorists, in order to understand the origins of the human fascination with sport, we need to see human nature in evolutionary context. Our prehistoric ancestors faced many **(1)** _____, and in order to survive, they needed to be hunters and fighters. Life was dangerous and **(2)** _____. However, the emergence of modern societies has enabled us to **(3)** _____*achieve*_____ a relatively greater degree of **(4)** _____ in our daily lives. One of the most notable features of most modern societies is the bureaucratic structure within government. A bureaucracy employs, (or is supposed to employ) very **(5)** _____ rules or **(6)** _____ in order to make a decision or determine a course of action within the bureaucratic organization. As bureaucracies extend into every major **(7)** _____ of society, our lives have become ever more **(8)** _____, at least in theory.

Many sports have an **(9)** _____ of risk that may not be present in our daily lives. Therefore, sport is motivated by the desire to **(10)** _____ some of the risk that civilized life has eliminated. According to this theory, the **(11)** _____ of any sport contest is generally unpredictable. Therefore, the passion that many of us exhibit for sport represents our desire to **(12)** _____ for the regularity and boredom of our bureaucratized lives by engaging in activities that still **(13)** _____ some of the elements of danger, excitement, and uncertainty characteristic of our evolutionary past. In other words, when life **(14)** _____ to provide us with reminders of our evolutionary past, we **(15)** _____ the past through participation in sport.

For Discussion

Discuss these questions with a partner or a small group.

1. Do you agree with Cashmore, that there is an instinctual basis for sports and that watching or playing sports serves a compensatory role in our lives? Why or why not? Can you think of any arguments to refute the author's explanation? Explain Cashmore's argument in your own words and then give your argument against this view.

2. Cashmore argues that life in contemporary society has become too safe, and participation in sports is our way of restoring some danger to our lives. Do you agree or disagree with this assessment? Explain why.

For Further Investigation

Choose one of these projects. Research the topic, and write a report or give a brief oral presentation of your findings.

1. Identify a particular group, for example, child athletes, college athletes, master's athletes, or participants in extreme sports, and try to find out what motivates people in this group to participate in sports. Use an academic library or Internet sources to collect background information. If possible, create and conduct a survey with a group or interview several participants.

2. One popular idea in the United States is that participation in sports builds character. This idea is hinted at in Paragraph 3 of Ellis Cashmore's "The Why of Sports," and it is an often-repeated theme in the popular press and among coaches and organizations that promote sports. Is there any evidence, based on careful research, that supports a connection between sports participation and character-building? Try to locate several academic sources that address this question and review the evidence and conclusions for the "sports builds character" theory.

3. Do you know of any activity, ancient or modern, in your own culture that might be considered by some people as a sport but by other people as not a sport? Using sources from a library or the Internet, identify such an activity. Make a brief written or oral report and share it with your classmates.